REINVENTING YOUR LIFE

Your guide to finding fulfillment in starting your business

SANDRA HUGHES

ISBN: 978-1-7337699-0-7 (paperback)
ISBN: 978-1-7337699-1-4 (e-book)

Website: https://lifereinvented.com

Email: sandra@lifereinvented.com

Facebook: https://www.facebook.com/ lifereinventedsandrahughes

LinkedIn: https://www.linkedin.com/in/lifereinvented

Copyediting by Author One Stop, Inc. (www.AuthorOneStop.com)

Design and production by Joanne Shwed, Backspace Ink (www.backspaceink.com)

Images by arip teguh santoso, Max4e Photo, and Findriyani

I would like to acknowledge:

My Love Graydon and daughters Elle and Cat
—for your love and constant encouragement.

Joanne Shwed, Randy Peyser, and Gail Martin
—for helping make this book happen.

Lori Bitter, Mary Furlong, Sunil Bhaskaran, Cassie Breegerman, Ellen Dorian, Maryanne Gucciardi, Beth Love, Cindy Manit, Jen McFarland, Katie Collins, Sarah Hadley, Candace Smith, Luci Gabel, Genet Simone, Alison Suggs, Allison Kinnear, Sharla Jacobs and Jesse Koren, Susan Matthews Scott, Tracy Cone, and Michael Koplin—for your continued support!

Contents

Introduction

You are about to set out on an exciting, fulfilling, frustrating, wonderful, frightening, and ultimately worthwhile journey as you create your new future. Regardless of your circumstance and where you want to go, this book can help you create an action plan that will minimize lost time and dead ends while enabling you to get off to the best possible start and increase your satisfaction and success.

Here are some questions to consider as you are contemplating this change or your new chapter:

- Have you been thinking about starting your own business?

- Are you considering a big shift in your career path?

- Are you leaving your job (e.g., retiring or downsizing) and thinking of a move into entrepreneurship?

- Do you want to leave your job but aren't sure how to create a better one?

- Are you looking for an active retirement that allows you to keep your hand in the game?

- Are you an early-stage entrepreneur who is considering pivoting in a new direction?

Ideally, you still have a job and are planning for a future change, or you are just about to leave or have recently left your job and are thinking about starting your own business.

Set the Stage

As a long-time business strategist, I've helped build businesses. Time and again, I've found that business owners who take time to plan ahead experience much less frustration and are ultimately happier with the results they achieve than those who don't.

Take a moment to think about what you want:

- How much income do you need?
- How much disposable income do you want?
- How long do you want to work?
- How long will you need to work?
- Are you excited about remaining in the same field, or are you ready to try something new?

Some of you may continue to work for a while and then make your move. Perhaps you've already started a business. Maybe you are just planning for the future. Regardless of your situation, it's good to start thinking about your options now. This book will suggest steps to take, choices to consider, and ideas of what's possible.

Before we get into the thick of things, here's some clarification about terminology. I'm going to use the terms "business" and "company" interchangeably. I realize that you may think of a "company" as a large corporation and a "business" as a smaller enterprise, like a consulting or service firm, an individual franchise, a multilevel-marketing venture, a solo practice, or a sole proprietorship. For the purposes of this book, and to keep from repeating the same term, "business" and "company" have the same meaning.

The action plan you'll create isn't a take-it-to-the-bank kind of document, although not much will have to be added to make it into that type of document. This plan is for *you*—helping you discover what you need to know about yourself, the industry, the marketplace, and your customers before you launch your new venture, so that you are positioned for the best chance of success. I'll also take you through the important steps to build a solid foundation for your business as you jump into creating a "sales funnel" to attract clients, so that you are better positioned to deliver what you promise.

You may think that planning sounds boring or frightening. However, with the methods I'll teach you in this book, it's actually an exciting chance to explore your unique aptitudes, delve into the industry in which you want to create your business, and figure out how to make this new enterprise everything you want it to be. You'll get clear about whether you want to have a business or a hobby.

Some of you may continue to work for a while and then make your move.

Along the way, you'll learn to get comfortable with the reality of needing to go out and attract clients. You'll also discover how to put a revenue target in place by figuring out how you will fill your sales funnel.

As you follow the steps in this book, you'll gain confidence, learn to anticipate and solve common problems *before* they slow you down, and avoid the pitfalls that can lead to disillusionment.

You'll be ahead of the competition, and the small, upfront investment in time will pay off many times over as you cruise to a more successful rollout.

The first 11 chapters have a few "next steps" questions for you to answer. They're meant to get you thinking, help you dig deeper into your assumptions and expectations, and lay the groundwork for your plan. The process is easy, insightful, and valuable. By the end of the book, your plan will be fleshed out and ready for you to run with it. If you want to delve deeper, a home-study course is available (https://lifereinvented.com/ programs/).

My goal is to help you go into your new business strong because you have thought everything through, considered your options, chosen a path, and fully understood the potential obstacles you may face. I will provide tools to help you decide if you really want to go out on your own. If you do want to do that, I will show you how to navigate the most common obstacles to lessen their impact. With your plan in hand, you'll feel confident and empowered, and you will be resilient when setbacks happen because you will anticipate them and know how to pivot in response while saving time, energy, and frustration.

I'm looking forward to making this journey with you. Congratulations on taking the first step toward your exciting new future!

CHAPTER 1

Get Started

Right now, you have a chance to do something that will vastly increase your odds for success as you start up your new business.

You can pause and take this time to make sure that your expectations, assumptions, experiences, needs, vision, and market are in alignment. It's the "ready, aim" before you "fire." As in marksmanship, this preparation can make all the difference in whether or not you hit the bull's-eye.

It can be extremely exciting to charge into action because you're busy and feel like you're doing *something*. However, if you go full tilt without a plan, you might make great time but not end at the expected and desired destination. I want to help you consider your options, so you can cover all your bases, think through your alternatives, and do your best to assure that your new business includes the things you love and doesn't replicate the things you don't.

Most importantly, this is your chance to align your new business with your life values and the parts of your previous career that brought you the most satisfaction. Whether you plan to work 10, 20, or more years, wouldn't it be wonderful to spend that time doing something you love, contributing in a ful-filling and valuable way, and leaving behind a legacy of good work?

Begin with a Pause

Stop now and think about what you liked the most—and dis-liked the most—about your previous jobs. Grab a piece of paper and answer these questions:

- What tasks and personal interactions brought you the most satisfaction?
- What outcomes gave you the most fulfillment?
- When did you feel "in the zone" and perform at your personal best?
- What was on your calendar on days when you woke up and felt excited to get to work?
- What types of people did you most enjoy working with, and what were your favorite interactions with them?

Some of these questions may be milestone accomplishments that you might put on a resume. Others are small, essential threads that make up the fabric of your everyday life and have an outsized effect on your overall happiness.

Now think about these questions differently, noting what made you feel frustrated, unhappy, or unfulfilled in previous jobs:

- What tasks and personal interactions brought you the most dissatisfaction?
- What outcomes gave you the least fulfillment?
- When did you not feel "in the zone" and not perform at your personal best?
- What was on your calendar on days when you woke up and felt less excited to get to work?

- What types of people did you least enjoy working with, and what were your least favorite interactions with them?

Take a look at the two lists. It might sound obvious, but it's amazing how often people don't stop to think about what they love (and hate) about their work and accidentally replicate the things they most disliked. You're in charge of your future, so why not plan from the start to create a business that best suits your unique strengths and complements the life you want to live?

Now is the time to assure that, in the business you are creating, you can have more good days than bad days by developing a structure that allows you to be at your best.

If you've always worked for a corporation or for someone else's company, take a moment to think about how you really feel, deep down, about self-employment. Our culture tends to assume that people will graduate from school and have a career as an employee rather than owning their own business. **Stop now and think about what you liked the most—and hated the most—about your previous jobs.** Sometimes we internalize attitudes about career choices without being conscious of our thought process.

Who Are You?

Try on the idea of describing yourself as "self-employed" or saying, "I own my own business." How does that make you feel? Confident? Proud? Excited? Or do you feel a little adrift, like you aren't part of a tribe anymore? There's no wrong answer.

If you aren't completely comfortable with thinking of yourself as self-employed, dig a little deeper and ask yourself why. Have you internalized negative assumptions or stereotypes about people who aren't part of a corporation? Maybe it's time to fact-check those ideas and revise your thinking, so that these concerns don't get in your way.

We're often programmed to describe ourselves with our job title. For many people, their title is a source of pride, status, and accomplishment. When you leave your old job, you also leave your title behind. Sure, your new title is "Owner/President," but are you completely comfortable with not having (being) the title you held before? Of course, we are always more than just a job title, but many of us have gotten attached to our title and the reaction it evokes from others. Do you feel strange or diminished without your old title?

Take a few moments and think about what you feel about your old title and how letting it go changes your comfort level in social situations or in the way you think about yourself. You want to be able to step into this new chapter in your life feeling confident and empowered, so watch out for little things like this that might need to be considered.

> **We're often programmed to describe ourselves with our job title.**

Now is a good time to get out of the habit of referring to what you do using a title. Instead, talk about the outcomes you create. Think about your last/current job and see if you can flip your title for an outcome. For example, instead of saying, "I'm a vice president of marketing," you'd say, "I inform the world how my business creates products and services to serve our customers and stakeholders." See the difference? Titles can mean many things, but when you put the emphasis on outcomes, you get the chance to shape how someone else sees you in a more customized and results-based way that shows what you *really* do.

When you focus on what you do and whom you serve, you create a more powerful introduction than by sharing a name and a title. You clearly position yourself in the mind of the person you've just met in terms of your niche market and the benefits you create. A what-you-do and who-you-serve introduction sets you apart and demonstrates your confidence and enthusiasm in a meaningful, memorable way.

Think about how giving up status or perks from your old/ current job affects the way you think about yourself:

- Does it bother you to not work in a big office building, to get your own health insurance, or to not have paid time off?

- Will you chafe at not being associated with a famous big-name company?

- Will you feel self-conscious about being frugal or feel like you've been demoted?

While such feelings might not be entirely logical, they're perfectly human.

Our society has trained us how to think, what to expect, and what to take for granted. When you find yourself emotionally attached to certain status symbols and luxuries, examine why they seem so important to you. "Deprogramming" from those conditioned desires means "rethinking" learned behaviors and questioning assumptions. The outcome of having the freedom to love what you do can be well worth the effort.

When your enthusiasm for what you're creating outweighs the benefits of your old job, small sacrifices are easy to take in stride. Be prepared to be struck at the most unlikely time with nostalgia for the parts of your old job that you liked or that made you feel important. Think about how best to bolster your confidence and reassure yourself that you are on the path to creating something better and more satisfying and that the trade-offs are worth it.

Plan Your End Game

While you're in a self-assessment mode, this is a good time to think about what you want to do in your retirement:

- Do you plan to quit working at some point and live the "good life"?

- Are you so excited about what you do that you may eventually scale back but plan to work as long as your health permits?

- Would you like to build up a business and then sell it for additional retirement income?

- How much money do you need to cover your expenses now? Do you expect this situation to change in retirement?

Part of matching your next-step career and your ideal retirement means working out your retirement budget. If you have a nest egg, a financial advisor can help you develop a plan to maximize returns while drawing out a "stipend" each year for living expenses. For some of you, what you earn from your new business will be on top of that retirement disbursement as well as Social Security, any pension you've earned, and any other stream of income, like rental properties.

You should be able to estimate both the disbursement (if any) from your investment nest egg and your Social Security/pension fairly accurately. How much of a shortfall is there between your essential costs and your predictable income? That number is what you would have to earn from your new business. If you can reduce your costs so that you cover your key expenses (e.g., housing, food, utilities, healthcare/insurance, and transportation) from your retirement nest egg, you will have less pressure to hit and maintain a critical level of income from your new business. On the other hand, now that you know which target costs must be covered, and if your business earns that much or more, you can stretch out your nest egg by not needing to draw on it as quickly.

Before you make a commitment, try living on your retirement budget. Did you forget to include important expenses? Are you chafing at giving up some luxuries? Think about what you can eliminate and what you still need. For those expenses that are difficult to jettison, ask yourself, "How do they define me?" You may have to uncover and identify a psychological need before you can decide whether or not you can live without that extra spending.

As you're planning, anticipate being part of the "sandwich" generation, which is caught between caring for older parents and having children going to college (or paying off your own student loan(s)). How might ailing parents or a rise in tuition affect your budget? Becoming a caregiver also impacts how much time and flexibility you have for your growing business. Anticipating life's speed bumps gives you more control over your future because you can make plans to deal with foreseeable obstacles.

Another question to ask yourself is, "How much do I need to be around people, and where will I get support?" Working from home keeps your overhead low and increases your profits, but the downside can be isolation. You can get some interpersonal connection via social media and phone calls, but think about **Part of matching your next-step career and your ideal retirement means working out your retirement budget.** other ways to create a supportive network of like-minded people with whom you can share your concerns and triumphs. Working with a mentor can be part of your support network and provide insights into business options.

Joining an existing group can give you a feeling of belonging if you find an organization that meets your needs. If you've met a handful of other entrepreneurs in noncompeting industries who seem to share your values and goals, consider putting together a mastermind group. This type of group meets on a regular basis (i.e., quarterly, monthly, or bimonthly). The members share, in confidence, their triumphs and obstacles, and help each other brainstorm ideas and make helpful connections. (We'll talk more about these types of mastermind groups in the book. For now, just let it plant a seed in your thoughts.)

Where a mastermind group is made up of your peers, creating your own informal board of directors can also be useful. In this case, you reach out to several people whom you admire and have gotten to know and who are ahead of you in their business success. Ask them if they will be your advisor in exchange for treating them to a nice restaurant meal quarterly. This kind of "board" isn't legally binding and doesn't have any oversight responsibilities. Instead, it's your chance to ask for advice and gain the insight of people who are willing to mentor you and give back to the business community.

As you move forward, realize that nobody knows everything. Don't feel shy about asking for information or help. Develop mutually beneficial relationships with others at your level, seek out mentors who are further ahead, and pay your debt forward by helping those with less knowledge than you.

 **NEXT STEPS**

1. Looking at your answers to the questions in this chapter, let them sit for a day and look at them again. Are you comfortable with your responses? Did you think of something that you wanted to add or change?

2. If your answers made you feel uncomfortable, sit with the feeling and examine the source of the discomfort. Are you sad about letting something go or apprehensive about moving toward it? It's okay to ease into a major life shift. Listen to what your feelings are telling you.

CHAPTER 2

Pause-Reflect-Reset

Y ou are creating a plan to help you stop and think before you dive into your new business. Enthusiasm and a good idea aren't enough by themselves to carry you through the transition. You need a 10,000-foot overview of what is involved, so you can anticipate challenges and adjust your course to avoid false or risky starts. My goal is to help you move forward with intention and avoid constant reactions to circumstances. Having a plan puts you in control.

Ideally, one-year, three-year, and five-year goals are good ideas. It's true that the further out you project, the more life is likely to require course corrections, but it's essential to have a destination in mind.

Pause-Reflect-Reset

Part of the pause-reflect-reset approach includes taking care of yourself during this transitional time. It's easy to bury feelings when you're busy. Step back and allow yourself to feel the shock of the major shift you're experiencing. This is especially necessary if the circumstances that require you to find a new career path are not entirely up to you (e.g., with a reorganization or a merger or while downsizing).

Sit quietly and let yourself feel. Anger, betrayal, disappointment, and sadness are all parts of the process of letting go. You invested a lot in your former life and stepping away isn't easy, particularly if you feel like the choice was not your own.

Even if you willingly chose to leave your prior job, sadness is still part of closure, no matter how excited you might be over your opportunities. It's normal to feel wistful and for a new beginning to be bittersweet. As with any grieving process, it's not a once-and-done thing.

> **Letting go is part of setting the stage for the next phase of your work life.**

Expect the feelings to come back, sometimes when you least expect it. Don't fight it. Embrace the emotions, let them wash over you, and realize that it's a way of honoring all the good things about the successes and friendships you built in that stage of your life.

Letting go is part of setting the stage for the next phase of your work life. As you transition from working for a corporation to working for yourself, you'll find that, over time, your friendship groups will shift. Many of our workplace friendships arise from proximity (and sometimes from shared adversity) instead of from common interests outside of work. Just as relationships with friends from high school and college may gradually drift away over time, so may work relationships. Sometimes values shift as you strive to better align your personal and business lives. In other cases, relationships may change due to a lack of ongoing shared experiences.

People who have never been outside the corporate environment may not understand or empathize with the challenges facing a business owner. Or you may find that the chatter about people you no longer work with isn't as interesting as it used to be, especially as more of your former colleagues' coworkers are people you don't know. Sadly, some people may also step away if you can no longer help them make connections inside the organization or do them favors. That's okay. You're building something new.

Create New Networks

Finding new friends, hobbies, and networking groups are an essential part of long-term success for a business owner. Some options may be found online, connecting you to people around the world who share your interests and are supportive of your goals. Make in-person friends to avoid the feelings of isolation that can be a surprise for those who find themselves working from home after decades of being surrounded by people in an office.

Networking, always important in corporate life, becomes vital once you're on your own. It's essential to network with intention, so you don't end up investing time and energy in groups that aren't a good fit for your ultimate goals. Don't make the mistake of rushing out and joining every business group you find. Look carefully at the group's organizational goals to see if they align with where you want to go. Attend a meeting and notice the professions and skill levels of the other attendees. Can these people provide referrals, be a resource or potential collaboration partner, or supply skills that you need to grow? Are they possible clients? If not, it isn't likely to be a good fit, so move on.

The goal is to find a few groups where you can build a strong, mutual support network. Ideally, you want to help the others in your group, just as you hope to be able to rely on them for help. Attend regularly, look for ways to help others without always getting something in return, and find opportunities to use your talents for the good of the group. In this way, you'll build trust and credibility.

When you leave the corporate life, you let go of more than your work friends. Your support system also changes. Instead of having information-technology personnel nearby to fix your computer, or human resources to handle your benefits, you will have to either learn new skills or find independent contractors to supply those needs. Part of your plan should include asking for referrals and vetting possible contractors before you have a crisis, so you already have phone numbers in hand when you need help.

Breaking Up Is Hard to Do

Intangible things are often the most difficult to let go (e.g., the status of having a special parking spot, a coveted office, or a paid vacation). Expectations can be surprisingly difficult to adjust, especially if at one time you hoped to make partner, be promoted to a particular title, or be rewarded with a company car, a large expense account, or a similar, visible, high-status perk. The psychological safety net of a steady paycheck is also hard to give up until you realize that, in today's uncertain corporate climate, no one's employment is safe or guaranteed. It can be difficult to let go of a routine that gives structure to your day, even if you hated your commute and like the idea of flexible work hours.

Leaving your old job and starting your own business means stepping out of your comfort zone. It's okay to admit that this prospect scares you. It means having to earn your credibility again with a new audience, perhaps even from scratch if you're doing something different. Here's the important part: Expect these feelings to be part of your transition. Make them a part of your plan, so you don't get discouraged, push too hard too fast, or give up too soon. It gets better!

Your plan should consider how you can transfer skills from your old job to your new business, where you can play to your strengths, and how to demonstrate what you're good at. Structure your business to take advantage of your strong points and outsource the parts you aren't good at or don't enjoy to people who excel in those areas. Realize that you will also grow into new skills and discover new abilities as you go along. If possible, easing into your new role is good because you will gain new competences and confidence as you go instead of flailing a bit when you dive in all at once.

Plan to experience a crisis of confidence somewhere along the way, often when you least expect it. Once the shock of making a big change wears off, you'll feel the newness and overwhelming feelings. For example, people tell me all the time, "I never thought I'd be starting over at 50." Beginning again and charting a new course can be daunting, but it's also liberating and exhilarating because it will teach you so much about yourself.

By taking the step to start over, you will find out who you are and what you really want. You will be the master of your destiny. So many of us choose our professions as teenagers, either drifting in the direction of classwork we don't hate or picking a job to make **Leaving your old job and starting your own business means stepping out of your comfort zone.** someone else (a parent, a teacher, or a mentor) happy, impress our friends, or yield to societal pressure. We are conditioned to follow expectations about prestigious schools and jobs with status, high salaries, and other impressive credentials.

At that young age, we don't know what we will find fulfilling or soul-sucking. This assessment won't happen until we are years down the road. Then we discover that, if we had to do it all over again, knowing what we know now, we'd do it differently.

This is your chance.

PAUSE. Then REFLECT. Think about what you love doing and what you hate, and what you're good at and what you never want to do again. Draw on the life experience and perspective you have gained over the years to look at work in a new way. Think about skills that you didn't learn in school (e.g., empathy, listening, and emotional intelligence). If you're still not clear on where your true strengths lie, ask people who know you well or sign up for skill and personality testing.

Traits that are strengths in one situation can sometimes be perceived as threatening in another environment or can even be counterproductive. It's time to unpack and identify judgments about your abilities and lay them on the table, so you can fully assess all the tools at your disposal as you begin this new chapter in your life. Can you flip the perspective and recognize that what might be positive in some situations (e.g., being stubborn) can be a hindrance in different circumstances? Or that what you might have been told was a negative trait (e.g., being outspoken) can actually be positive? That's part of the RESET.

> **Traits that are strengths in one situation can sometimes be perceived as threatening in another environment or can even be counterproductive.**

In Chapter 3, we'll talk more about how to align your strengths in your plan so that you can feel fulfilled with your new career path. Keep reading ... we're getting to the good part!

NEXT STEPS

1. Make one list of traits that you consider to be your strengths and another list of your weaknesses. Look at each list and think of circumstances that would flip the script (i.e., make a strength into a weakness and a weakness into a strength). Does thinking about traits from two different vantage points change your perspective?

2. Think about your work friends and your current networking groups. With whom do you want to stay in contact, either because you've got a genuine personal connection or because you can be helpful to each other? Try to nurture those connections once you no longer share an employer. Which networking organizations are just for employees of big corporations? Which groups actively support and promote professionals who are self-employed? Those are the groups to keep on your short list and cultivate.

 **FOOD FOR THOUGHT**

Look Before You Leap!

Sally, one of my clients, was moving to another state. She decided to go for professional certification as a therapist in the new state and started accumulating hours toward that goal. During our coaching sessions, Sally realized that, while she had earned the hours necessary, getting the certification would actually create more limits for what she could or couldn't offer her clients than what she could do for them at that time. She decided to become a counselor and considered coaching training.

Up-front planning can save time and effort. While no education is ever truly wasted, Sally could have spent the funds that she invested in getting that certification (and the time involved) in ways that would have benefitted her more.

Sometimes we fall in love with the idea of having a degree, a certification, or some other milestone, and we don't really consider the tangible benefits. It's nice to have another certificate on the wall, but how will it help you get more clients or earn more revenue?

CHAPTER 3

Stay Focused

When you begin to plan your new business, it's easy to go down one rabbit hole after another, becoming distracted and anxious over the possibilities of all there is to consider.

Some would-be business owners go off like a rocket, energized and excited about their new venture. However, without planning, that excitement can fizzle as obstacles they haven't anticipated pop up and slow them down. Others want to plan before jumping in but don't know how. My hope is that this book will help both kinds of people find what they need to be successful.

It's important to remain focused, but it's essential to be focused on the right things. How do you know what those "right things" are? Your plan, with its timeline and prioritized bullet points, will help you keep your attention where it needs to be.

It's also essential to watch out for the most common focus busters that trip up new business owners. Here are three to consider:

Focus Buster #1: Tasks vs. Big Picture

People may say, "Don't get so busy working *in* your business that you forget to work *on* your business." In other words, don't get so wrapped up going from task to task that you forget to get out there and attract business.

There will be a million and one things to do in your start-up business. Since you are likely to be the sole employee, you'll feel pressured to do all of them. Be careful not to get so trapped in the minutiae that you forget about networking, creating alliances and collaborations, laying the foundation for the next expansion of products or services, or marketing your expertise and growing your client base.

The time to look ahead and gain new clients is when you're crazy-busy serving the ones you have. If you wait until you have all your tasks completed, you may find that the pipeline for new work has dried up while you were busy. It's a juggling act but something to consider as you budget your time. It's like taking a road trip and being so focused on the mile markers that you forget to take your exit or lose track of where you're going. Being a business owner requires a dual focus for tasks and strategy that are always competing for your attention and time.

What tasks do you find so enjoyable or engrossing that they tempt you to get sucked in and lose sight of the big picture? Which items on your to-do list are you dodging or procrastinating about doing? Busyness can be a way of avoiding responsibilities that make us uncomfortable or that we don't enjoy. Can you alternate tasks you like with those that aren't your favorite, so you don't feel stuck doing things you dislike?

Focus Buster #2: Perfectionism

Are you a person who believes that "good enough" is never good enough? While your attention to detail might be admirable in some situations, realize that perfectionism can also be a way to dodge doing other tasks that you want to avoid.

No one can fault you for wanting to make something as good as it can be, right? It depends on whether that extra 10 percent of focus actually makes a difference or whether that time and effort could have been spent on something else with no discernible differ-

Are you a person who believes that "good enough" is never good enough?

ence in quality. This principle is called "diminishing returns," meaning that, after a certain point, extra effort doesn't yield enough of an improvement to be worth the additional work. If you let yourself get caught up in doing more than necessary all the time, you'll find that you're expending time, energy, resources, and focus without seeing a substantial payoff.

Perfectionism can also be a coping method to deal with anxiety. Deep down, are you scared about making the jump to a new career or worried about finances? Throwing all your focus into making things absolutely perfect can be a way to keep yourself distracted, so that you don't have to deal with the anxious feelings. Unfortunately, it's a short-term fix that causes long-term problems. Perfectionism can redirect your energy to comfortable, but less important, tasks and leave you too tired or emotionally drained to tackle essential responsibilities that are out of your comfort zone.

Perfectionism often hides a fear of failure. It's okay to be anxious, worried, and uncertain as you make a big life change. You're not the only one who feels these emotions on the journey to starting your own business. In fact, as you cope with market changes and other shifting dynamics, you'll feel uncomfortable time and again. It goes with the job. That's why it's so important to recognize when your coping mechanisms might actually be undermining your progress.

Networking with people who have the same kinds of concerns can ease your worry. Everyone faces the same uncertainty, lack of confidence, and fears. Your networking partners can include your coach, a mastermind group, a business support circle, or other trusted business allies. Hearing stories from those who might be further along in their success (e.g., how they felt at your stage of the game and what still makes them feel anxious) might make you feel more confident once you realize that you're not the only one to have those feelings. You may learn some new coping tips on how to redirect your anxiety into more productive outlets rather than spinning your wheels to be perfect.

Perfectionism can often mask a fear of change. We all like comfortable routines and certainty. However, today's world is constantly changing. Running a successful business requires being able to tweak, adapt, pivot, and shift to remain competitive and relevant. You can't afford to get stuck in a rut, no matter how comfortable it feels at the moment.

Focus Buster #3: Business, Part-Time Job, or Hobby?

Do you want a business, or are you looking for a hobby or a part-time job? Think carefully about your stage of life and the time you want to devote. Aside from whether or not the Internal Revenue Service considers your new endeavor to be a "real" business or a hobby (based on the advice of a professional regarding income generated and profitability), how much do you want to give to this new creation?

Here's another way to think about it: Do you want the responsibility of parenting a newborn to adulthood, or would you rather be the grandparent or a favorite aunt or uncle? Are you up for all the late-night emergencies and total focus, or would you rather just drop in for the highlight reel? Building something that's going to be a real business takes total commitment while a hobby can be more relaxed because you're not as invested (or dependent) on the ongoing outcome. Having a business requires creating revenue targets and endeavoring to meet them.

This shift may be the first time you've ever had the chance to think about who you are and what you want without worrying about pleasing parents, mentors, or society. Do you feel that you have to have a full-time job because

Do you want a business, or are you looking for a hobby or a part-time job?

that's what "they" expect (or what your internalized expectations demand)? Are you at a point in life where you have the resources to take time off either for good or at least for a while? If so, do you really want to launch a new business, or would you rather dabble at something that strikes your fancy without pressure or expectations?

It's okay to just want a hobby. In fact, some people begin what they think of as a hobby, and it eventually grows into a full business. There's nothing wrong with taking an artisan approach and pursuing an interest to see where it goes if your finances and situation allow.

Obviously, this type of arrangement works better for some kinds of businesses than others. If you're in a field that requires licensure, continuing education, or other official requirements, or one that is more service-based than product-oriented, the hobby approach probably won't be an option. However, if you are thinking about doing something as a creative outlet and seeing what comes of it, backing into a business by starting it as a hobby might be a good way to increase your enjoyment and decrease your stress.

If you start with a hobby instead of a business, it's going to affect your timeline and priorities. You might be able to put off some of the "less fun" aspects for a while until your "hobby" expands beyond your own enjoyment.

For example, suppose you decide to make homemade soap, throw pottery, or bake cookies. You invest your time and effort into trial and error, developing or tweaking recipes and trying new techniques. As you gain skills, you start to share your output as gifts. Friends and family urge you to sell what you make, and you've already outstripped your needs and what your friends can use.

At that point, you're looking at transitioning from a hobby to a business. **The best part? The next step is up to you!** You'll still need to create a plan and think through the issues we've already discussed, but you've had time to ease into the situation. Or you may decide to keep what you're doing as your recreation and give away or donate your creations. The best part? The next step is up to you!

NEXT STEPS

1. Do you recognize any of the three focus busters as things you might be prone to doing? How have you kept those tendencies from derailing you in the past? How might you make sure that they don't trip you up now?

2. Take extra time to consider the "hobby vs. job" question. Be honest with yourself. What are you looking for? What do you need? What would make you happy? Are you ready to set revenue targets and work toward them? There is no wrong answer, but you'll remain more in sync with yourself as you move forward if you are clear about what you want.

CHAPTER 4

Set Priorities

With so many possibilities, how do you know where to start? Begin by prioritizing what you want to accomplish, which is part of creating your one-, three-, and five-year goals.

As you figure out your business priorities, you'll sort through your life values as well. When your values/priorities in life and business align, you'll feel less stress and more energy, and that awful sense of being pulled in different directions will go away.

Start with Research

Good information helps you make good decisions. Dig into facts and figures to explore the business environment you're planning to enter. Too often, we think that we can go with what we "know" or with our gut feeling. Unfortunately, what we think we know is often a mishmash of things we've read online or heard people say, which may be out of date or mistaken. While your intuition or "gut feeling" can be valuable, it needs accurate data to be reliable.

If you've always worked for someone else, especially if you haven't been in a management position, some of the topics in this book may be new to you. If you've been in a management role, human resources (HR) and finance staff have probably handled these issues for you. Now that you're starting your own business, you'll need to develop relationships with qualified people who can keep you compliant with the laws and out of trouble.

Why do you need to think about all these things when you just want to dive in and get going? As the saying goes, "Well begun is half done." Taking the time at the start to do research and line up your expert helpers will save you time, money, headaches, and legal problems down the road.

Get the Fundamentals Right

What kinds of things do you need to research? Let's start with the basics. In order to succeed and make wise decisions, you need to learn everything you can about your industry and the market for your kind of product(s) as well as your customers and competitors. It's important to understand how others are pricing their competing services/products and how your plan differs from the competition.

Is the market for what you want to provide growing, stable, shrinking, or in chaos? Who are your competitors (e.g., locally, regionally, nationally, and globally)? What's been going on in your industry lately (e.g., legal issues, big players entering or leaving the market, scandals, or consumer relations)? If there are big, messy issues brewing, you want to know about them, so you can avoid repeating others' mistakes or accidentally getting entangled.

Who are your customers? Where are they getting their products/services now, and why should they switch to you? Do they know that they need what you want to provide? Most importantly, what does your potential customer want? Focus on their needs and not on what you think they need. Businesses fail because they don't provide what their customers genuinely want. Is what you're offering so new that no one has it and your target market doesn't yet want it? The more details you can learn about your ideal customers, the better you'll be able to tailor your product, pricing, and delivery to their needs.

How do you do this research? If you're already associated with a professional or an industry association, take advantage of their salary surveys, networking opportunities, and other useful resources. Start with free online studies and articles from respected magazines, business organizations, and universities. Always check to see who published the material, and make sure you know whether they are reliable or whether they are driving an agenda for a special-interest group.

Is the market for what you want to provide growing, stable, shrinking, or in chaos?

See what local business groups offer in terms of market studies and industry overviews. Some organizations compile and update such data annually. While it may be pricy, this information is likely to be well researched and accurate. If you think the cost of information is high, just think about the price of big mistakes based on bad data. Don't skimp on the important things!

As you're studying your competition, pay attention to their marketing as well as their pricing and products. What kind of website do they have? Are they active on social media? If so, what social-media sites are they using to reach customers? What kind of promises do they offer? What guarantees, warranties, and return policies do they provide? What testimonials and case studies do they include, and what do their customers say about them? Check out independent review sites as well to get a more rounded opinion and perhaps uncover their weaknesses or your opportunities to fill a service gap. Now you can begin to think about the product(s) or service(s) you will provide that differentiate you from others and fill a void with something your potential customers/clients want.

Then you can apply my signature ADD framework: ANTICIPATE market needs, DIFFERENTIATE with a unique point of view, and DISRUPT by being innovative. By applying this framework, you can stay ahead of your competitors, offering unique and appealing product(s) to a market whose needs you have researched and matched and innovating enough to create a space for yourself among entrenched providers.

Save yourself a world of hurt and big expenses by learning up front about taxes and related government issues.

As you research, make sure you organize the information, so you can refer to it when you have questions. Printed material can go into files or binders sorted by subject. Websites can be bookmarked and organized by online folders, so they don't become a big jumble of links. A little organization up front will save you hours of searching later.

Save yourself a world of hurt and big expenses by learning up front about taxes and related government issues. You'll need to tell the Internal Revenue Service what kind of company structure you have created (e.g., a sole proprietorship, a professional partnership, a limited liability corporation, a personal assistant, or an S Corporation). Look into the basics of business licenses and insurance.

The structure of your business has tangible tax and legal ramifications, so it's important to know your options and understand how the choices affect your future income and flexibility. It's well worth it to consult with a professional in addition to what you learn via books, courses, or online data. Think of it as building a sturdy foundation for everything you want to achieve.

Program Objectives Recap

Let's recap your program objectives:

> Business Clarity + Annual Goals + Systems and Structure + Progress Monitoring = Business Plan + Strategy

This "equation" is the heart of this book and what I hope you will take away from having read it. Couple this with the need to Pause-Reflect-Reset, and you gain the mindfulness to move in intention and not reactivity.

Give Some Thought to Your Team

No one builds a successful business entirely by themselves. Think about how many people it took your former employer to provide the services/products they offered. You may not need to have employees at the beginning, but don't try to do everything yourself. This approach is a recipe for burnout. In today's complex world, it's impossible to be an expert about everything, especially about subjects as complicated as taxes, intellectual property law, and HR legal issues.

How do you find good team members? Ask other business owners for referrals to vendors whom they respect and trust. Listen when people warn you about someone shady or who provides poor service. Check online rating services and websites that report professional misconduct and malpractice judgments. Forewarned is forearmed!

Who might your team of experts include? Here are some ideas to get you started:

- **CPA:** Consult with an accountant who understands small business taxes and can provide advice on important tax-related issues.

- **Attorneys:** You will need legal help to set up your business structure; protect your intellectual property; trademark your logo and products; patent your inventions; set up your hiring contracts, nondisclosure/confidentiality/noncompete agreements, and review contracts; and provide advice to keep you out of trouble. It's unlikely that one person (or even one firm) will offer all these types of legal expertise, so be prepared to shop around to compile a list of legal advisors. Make sure to take advantage of online services that provide legal forms and limited legal advice, which can be great starting points.

- **HR:** Stay out of trouble by knowing what the law requires regarding wage and hour regulations, exempt/nonexempt employees, overtime, and other aspects of management. Make sure you understand the current definitions of "discrimination" and "sexual harassment," so that you don't find yourself in hot water. You can't rely on what was common or tolerated by former employers because many companies have toxic cultures. Stay true to your values by creating a safe and healthy environment for yourself and for anyone you hire.

  > Make sure you understand the current definitions of "discrimination" and "sexual harassment," so that you don't find yourself in hot water.

- **Benefits administration and payroll:** Even if you begin as a one-person business, you'll need health insurance for yourself, your life partner, and your dependents. Buying your own health insurance can be tricky, but there are ways to reduce your costs and take some expenses out of pretax dollars. Think about dental and vision insurance, life insurance, long-term disability insurance, and insurance coverage for your home office or place of business. If you hire staff, a benefits administration expert can help you avoid problems by setting up and managing the benefits you offer to your employees. Likewise, a payroll expert can make sure that you pay your employees and contractors on time, assure that deductions are correct, and handle W-2 and 1099 filings and other pay-related tasks.

- **Mentor:** Having someone who knows the ropes and can advise you when you hit a snag can help you avoid problems and give you valuable peace of mind. Consider your mentor to be a key part of your team.

- **Estate and succession planning:** Your new business will become an asset with an impact on inheritance and your retirement. Knowing how to structure key elements from the start can make it much less complicated and expensive if and when the time comes to sell or dissolve your business. Consult a reputable financial planner who specializes in working with small business owners to avoid costly problems down the line.

- **Banker:** Your new business will need a separate bank account and perhaps a credit card and line of credit. Someone at your local bank or credit union can advise you, set up your accounts, and walk you through the processes if and when you need to secure a business loan. It's best to develop and nurture a relationship with a contact/institution over time before you need them to lend you money.

Who takes care of you while you are busy taking care of business? Your team ideally includes people who can help you align your mental and physical health as well as your business needs, so that you can create and live your best life.

Beyond your healthcare professionals, your wellness team might include a fitness coach, workout partners, instructors for hobby activities that help you destress, a therapist/counselor to help you work through old baggage, a nutritionist, or people who help you "outsource" personal tasks (e.g., a cleaning service, a meal-preparation service, and a lawn service). Don't overlook the importance of taking time away from work with family, friends, and pets! You will function best when your personal and professional lives are balanced. Take time to take care of yourself, and don't fall behind in your nonwork commitments.

Don't be afraid to ask your team for help before you feel overwhelmed or things get out of control. Being proactive is much better than reacting after things start to go wrong. Your team will/should evolve as your business grows because the challenges and needs will change as your company becomes larger or more complex.

Bust Common Start-up Assumptions

How can you keep your overhead low as you create your new business?

One way to cut expenses is by questioning your assumptions. You have a choice of how you structure your work environment, so don't just go with what you're used to doing because it's familiar. There are often better, more convenient, and less expensive alternatives that quickly come to mind if you take the time to think about your options.

How much can you do from home? Do you really need to rent office space? This is a big money-saver but one that some new business owners don't stop to seriously consider. Having an office doesn't make you "official" or make your business any more "real." Are you looking for validation by having a ritzy office or by trying to impress people? Do you feel like you need to save face with former coworkers? Be attuned to your "inner game" and understand why you consider an office to be so important.

There can be bona fide reasons to have a separate space for your business. Maybe you need room for inventory or production activities. Perhaps you need to meet with clients in person and want to guard the privacy of your home. Having clients or employees park at your house can cause problems in many neighborhoods. Even if you decide that you do need a professional space to meet clients, explore all your choices before jumping into an expensive, difficult-to-change lease.

Challenge the assumption that you must meet in person. A large percentage of business can be done remotely via phone or inexpensive videoconferencing (like Zoom). These options save you and your customer commuting **How much can you do from home? Do you really need to rent office space?** time and expand your reach far beyond local driving distances. Do you need to store large amounts of material and tie up space (and money) in inventory? Are there just-in-time options that might work better and give you more flexibility? Do you really need to hire anyone right away? If you do need help, can you work with a part-time virtual assistant who works remotely?

Can you meet clients at a coffee shop or restaurant instead of your own conference room? Plenty of people use these "third-space" places to meet and do work. If you need more privacy, consider exploring shared, coworking office space that rents by the day or hour. Can you access shared production space? For example, many start-up producers of food items rent space and time at a commercial kitchen facility to prepare, package, and store their products in lieu of investing in their own restaurant and to comply with health codes.

How will you handle running into former colleagues/vendors/coworkers/customers? Think ahead about how you want to reposition yourself in their eyes, so they can become allies, resources, referral sources, and supporters. Expect some initial discomfort—both for you and for them. Plan how you can take the lead by stating what you do with confidence. Have a short elevator pitch ready and expect it to change over time. Don't get hung up on titles. Focus on the outcomes you produce and whom you serve.

Throughout this process, where you start out is not where you end up ... and that's okay. If you've never experienced setbacks in your life or work, the process may seem daunting to you because starting up a business is full of situations that require you to rethink, reevaluate, back up, pivot, or change direction. Focus on your inner resilience. You have gotten through challenges before, and you can do it again. Remember that it's easier to be resilient with a strong foundation. Careful planning helps minimize the unexpected problems that require adjustment and reaction.

It's not possible to maintain balance all the time. Life will have you dialing one side or the other, up or down. Create a healthy goal of achieving an average balance over the course of a week, a month, or a year. Neither your personal life nor your work life should get the short end or constantly make trade-offs or sacrifices.

NEXT STEPS

1. Go back to the suggestions of whom your business and personal team might include. List those functions, and then fill in the names of the people with whom you already have a relationship (e.g., your CPA or primary care physician). Look at the empty spaces and ask for referrals to build your team.

2. Sitting down with your life partner to talk about your new business doesn't have to be dry and boring. Consider making it a fun event, perhaps part of a weekend getaway or a nice dinner out. Back into the conversation by talking about hopes, dreams, and assumptions for the future. Then explore how your new business plans can help make those dreams come true for both of you!

FOOD FOR THOUGHT

Do You Really Need to Add More Square Footage to Provide More Value to Your Clients?

My client Brian, a high-performance personal trainer, saw a dramatic improvement in his business once he learned to set boundaries around payment and scheduling, which enabled him to cover his expenses and pay himself a salary. Things were going very well.

Without first doing research and planning, Simon added square footage to his studio and bought more equipment. However, these changes didn't yield enough additional revenue to outweigh the costs. He was behind on his rent, had to move out and sell the equipment, and started sharing space and equipment in someone else's studio.

Was he wrong to want to enhance his services to clients? Not at all. However—and this is important—if he had done some research, he probably would have discovered that these types of changes would increase his costs without increasing his profits. In the end, the changes he made to his business (i.e., purchasing additional equipment and adding additional space) did not result in any noticeable return on his investment. He could have polled his clients to see whether they would be willing to pay extra for access to the new equipment or surveyed his mailing list to see what people actually wanted.

Planning includes doing basic research that can save you expense and heartache. Planning also means doing simple math to figure out how many new clients you'd need to cover the cost of what you want to do. In Simon's case, he would have discovered that he'd either need to increase prices for his exist-ing customers or get an unrealistic number of new customers to end up in the black. Planning helps you be intentional, not reactionary.

Plan first and avoid big problems!

CHAPTER 5

Evaluate Options

Why are you thinking about starting your own business? Maybe you've been downsized or decided to retire from your previous employer and line of work. Or maybe you've come into a windfall that allows you the freedom to design your own course.

Perhaps you've relocated or need flexibility to adapt to other life changes. Maybe you're bored and want a new challenge. Perhaps you aren't happy with your current income or you're looking for an opportunity to grow professionally and make your own future.

Identifying your reason for becoming a business owner may help to shape what you choose to do and how/where/when you choose to do it. As we've discussed in previous chapters, you'll want to keep the best things about your prior positions and design your new business to avoid the parts you didn't like or that didn't bring out the best in you and in the people around you.

Do you want this new job to be full time or a side gig? We've touched on this question before, so let's explore the options more fully. After all, you want to make the most of your new fresh start!

Option #1: The Case for a Side Gig

When you decide to build your new business in your spare time, it allows you to keep the job you have (or get another paying job) to cover expenses as you lay the groundwork for your next step. Working on your new venture part-time lets you gain skills, network, set up your systems, and start attracting clients while building your business at a reasonable pace to weather the initial ramp-up period with a cushion of outside income.

> If you're still working for an employer, and you want to do something related to your current line of work, watch out for noncompete agreements.

Do you already know that you'll be making a big life change? Perhaps you know for certain that your current job is going away due to a merger, retirement, or relocation. You may be anticipating a big shift (e.g., divorce, health challenges, or a new child). Start small but begin soon, so you have time to prepare while earning useful extra income.

If you're still working for an employer and you want to do something related to your current line of work, watch out for noncompete agreements. Did you sign a noncompete agreement when you first took the job, which limits the kind of work you can do or where you can work (e.g., the types of firms or geographic locations)? These agreements often include a time limit for how long you have to wait to do similar work within that geographic boundary. Make sure you know what you've agreed to, so you don't end up with an unhappy surprise. Make sure your employer doesn't prohibit moonlighting.

If you can't start working part-time while you're employed, you can still make progress toward your goal. Do research, get training, or complete required certification. Read books, attend seminars, and begin networking to make connections, find resources, and learn more about your market. You may also be able to volunteer or work as an unpaid apprentice to make sure that you actually like doing the work.

Here are some other questions to ask about starting your business as a side gig:

- How much time do you have outside of work/family/ sleep/chores? Do you really have time to make a solid start on your new venture?

- From where can you work? As we mentioned before, don't assume that you have to jump into leasing space. Can you work from home in a spare bedroom or even a large closet? Depending on the type of work, you might be able to rent space in another facility by the hour or use a shared workspace. Some workers (e.g., hair stylists, tattoo artists, masseuses, and acupuncturists) can rent their "chair" space within a larger licensed facility. Some retail stores rent interior floor space/bays to smaller retailers. Finding a synergistic partner (i.e., someone whose business compliments yours instead of competing) might create nontraditional options for office/workspace, events, and promotion.

- What is your time worth? As you're developing your network and building relationships (or joining groups), be selective. Look for quality instead of quantity and learn how to say "no" politely to groups that aren't a good fit or want too much of your time. Determine a per-hour dollar amount for your time, and then use that amount to help you decide whether an event, an invitation, or an activity is "worth" your time.

- Which groups might be a good fit for now? Which groups might be better later on? As you network, you may find that some groups are great for helping you in the early stages because they're geared toward helping new businesses. They might eventually become less useful when you have your feet on the ground and have gained more experience. Likewise, you might feel put off by other groups that focus on established businesses because their emphasis isn't on the concerns you face right now. Remember them for later as your needs and interests evolve.

Option #2: Jumping in Feet First

Before you decide to leave your old job (or forego getting another job when your current employment ends), ask yourself some important questions:

- Do you have the resources to cover expenses while you ramp up your new business from scratch? This process can take months (or longer) before you have enough of a customer base to pay your bills.

- How many of your existing skills transfer to your new line of work? If you need to get certified, earn a license, do an apprenticeship, or just gain new competencies, you might want a job to cover expenses while you learn.

- How much of your existing business network of customers, colleagues, vendors, resources, and referral sources will follow you? Making a shift to do the same work independently may mean that you have a customer base already in place. Other people may need to network in an entirely different industry or location, which takes time.

- Do you need to get a new degree, gain certifications/licenses, or take out loans? Look before you leap and potentially save yourself time and money by avoiding extras you don't actually need. Always make sure that the institutions you deal with are accredited. Check their references thoroughly to avoid scams.

Option #3: Franchises

Consider franchising. Franchises make it possible to buy into a successful concept and duplicate a profitable business model without having to start from scratch. This option can shorten the time to get up and running and provide people and a handbook to guide you every step of the way. On the downside, some franchises are expensive. If you're used to doing things your own way, you might find franchise rules and streamlined systems restrictive. It's a turnkey solution that works well for some but not for others. Exploring this option in detail is beyond the scope of this book. If you're interested, however, do your research before making any commitments.

Now that you've made it through some of the basic decisions, it's time to plan your start!

NEXT STEPS

1. As you think about the three options discussed in this chapter, does one of them feel like a natural fit? Are you attracted or repelled on a gut-instinct level? Explore your reactions to see why you like or dislike a choice. Choose or eliminate options based on intuition and information.

2. You may find other options that suit you better. If there's an existing family business, you might have a built-in new career path. Have you already devoted years to a craft or hobby, building skills and a network of fellow devotees? Take a look at your "hobby" with fresh eyes to see if it's really a business opportunity in disguise.

FOOD FOR THOUGHT

Exit Strategy or Long-Term Plan?

My client Tom came to me because he was sure that he wanted to leave his tech job in two years to teach and consult. He didn't have any experience with either teaching or consulting, but they sounded more appealing given his frustrations with his current job.

As we began to work on a plan, Tom realized that teaching night classes part-time while keeping his day job might be a good way to build experience and see if he really enjoyed teaching as much as he thought he would. If he liked teaching, and once he had validated that part of his exit plan, Tom could begin researching what he'd need to make a successful shift and start working on any necessary certifications or training required in that field.

Part of the planning process involved looking at his cash flow and anticipating income and expenses. Once Tom worked out the numbers, he realized that it made more sense to stay in his job while he made plans for the future. He could receive a steady paycheck while he tried teaching and use his current income to pay for any preparation he'd need for teaching or consulting without putting his lifestyle in jeopardy. With a plan in place, Tom controlled how quickly or how long it took to reach his goal. He could accelerate his preparations to jump ship if he really hated his current job. Or he could enjoy the benefits and steady income while he prepared to make his dream a reality at some point in the future, maybe after he retired.

Planning put Tom in control of his future and helped him avoid jumping into a big shift before he had thought through all the ramifications.

Contrast Tom's story with that of another client. Sarah started a business without a plan in place after she left her nonprofit job. Two years later, she decided to do something different and give up her business because it was not what she really wanted.

In hindsight, Sarah wished that she had put a plan in place when she first started, which might have helped her avoid a costly detour of time and money. She realized that her journey did not have to be so difficult, especially since she ultimately saw ways to retain her prior income while building a new business on the side. Her new direction was in much better alignment with her personal goals, which was something she would have realized sooner if she had stopped to plan at the very beginning.

Another client named Judy took a severance package and left her corporate job to start her own business. She didn't stop to plan up front. Three years after starting her business, she decided that it wasn't meeting her needs, including income, and went back to a corporate job.

After some reflection, Judy understands that having a reliable source of income is essential while you're ramping up your new business. She wished that she and I had worked together from the beginning because it would have saved her from jumping in without an income safety net. Judy is now planning to rebuild her business as a side gig while she is still employed, thus making the leap when the new business is capable of supporting her.

Planning works, and it can save you a ton of time, money, and frustration. As they say in carpentry, "Measure twice, cut once"!

CHAPTER 6

Plan Your Fresh Start

Starting over can be exciting, but it can also make you feel vulnerable. Our identity is often tied to our experiences, so wading into new experiences can be daunting. Although you have certain knowledge and expertise, you can make the best of your uncertainty by being open to learning what you don't know or haven't yet mastered.

Pick Your Best Guide

Are you nervous about going it alone and worried about how to pick the best guide? Both feelings are natural and normal. Nervousness is part of doing something new, but it can spur you on rather than hold you back.

- How are you feeling about starting your new career plan?

- Do you think that you might need someone to help you identify and narrow down possibilities or uncover how to transfer your existing skills?

- Are you having difficulty getting your arms around the big picture and finding a path through all the items on your to-do list?

- Do you feel like you've got a good grip on the basics? Might it be helpful to have an experienced someone available for periodic questions and accountability?

Finding a mentor who is a good fit early in the process of starting your new business can be a huge help. They can assist you to avoid pitfalls and sidestep obstacles. A skilled guide can help you better understand your goals and set a course to achieve them.

In my experience, people who choose to work with a qualified, experienced mentor will approach the planning process more confidently and explore options and resources they might never have discovered on their own. As someone whose expertise falls more in line with mentoring (e.g., an experienced teacher who can provide insight), I believe that having a guide decreases anxiety and more quickly identifies both strengths and potential problems.

Make Research an Adventure

Learning what you don't know comes with the territory of starting up a business. Does the idea of digging through books and charts put you to sleep? Or would you rather plow through reports at your own speed rather than watch a video or attend a class? Does the idea of rolling up your sleeves and trying part of your new career excite you or make you want to run the other way?

Research is an essential part of the planning process. If the word "research" makes you think of boring school assignments, think again. Learning more about something that interests you can be creative and exciting. As you dig deeper into your new career choice, you'll find all kinds of unexpected things—some good, some cautionary, but all important. You'll uncover crucial nuggets that will help you stand out from the competition and provide exceptional service. It's like panning for gold!

One way to make research more fun is to determine what kind of learner you are. Do you like to read? Or do you prefer to listen as someone explains it to you? Do you pick up something faster by doing it a few times or by carefully studying the instructions? A coach can help you identify

Finding a mentor who is a good fit early in the process of starting your new business can be a huge help.

your best learning style (if you don't already know it) and steer you toward research resources that appeal to your best method for absorbing information. This approach doesn't mean that you won't go out of your comfort zone sometimes, but discovering ways to learn that match your preferred style can take some of the drudgery out of a vital step toward your future success.

Begin your research by validating the real average income for your new career. Don't rely on hearsay or the experiences of one or two people. The media often features people who are the exception, not the rule. So, if you base your projections on one or two interviews or blog posts, you might not see the whole picture. Use professional organizations, government and census statistics, and industry data to figure out the most likely income range for someone in the role you'd like to fill. Network with other people who do what you do, build connections, and get information about what they do and how they do it.

After your research, consider these questions:

- How does the new information compare to what you had in mind?

- Does it confirm what you'd hoped or give you reason to pause and reconsider?

- Can you live on an income in that range (knowing that, when you start out, you're more likely to be at the bottom of the scale)?

- How much adjustment will it take to live on that income?

- Will you be able to feel good about yourself if the income is much less than you were making in your old job?

- Can you meet your existing obligations?

- How will your partner or family feel about the change?

- Will it require giving up things that are important to you or them?

Most people don't start out at the top pay scale when they work for an employer. It can take decades to climb the corporate ladder and earn raises and benefits. When you transfer your skills to a new career or your own business, you might not start at the bottom again (although, if you're making a big switch, it's possible), but you probably won't be at the very top for a while.

When you look at an average income range, try to find out the full scale, so you know the lowest low and the highest high. Then see if you can find the percentage of people earning at each level. This data can save you from a "false middle" where a few high flyers skew the range high. While we all want to believe that we're the exception, it takes a little while to realistically get your feet under you in a new career. Plan to hit the middle or low-middle part of the range. If all goes well, and you exceed the plan, celebrate!

Educate Your Support Team

As you put your plan in place and learn more about what it takes to get your new business/career off the ground, educate your family and friends. Helping them have factual and realistic expectations will make it easier for them to support you. Be willing to step back and take time to figure things out. Talk about and share what you need to learn and what you've already discovered.

If your partner and all your friends have only worked for big corporations (or have been an employee but not a business owner), they won't automatically understand the challenges you are facing or the need to gather new information. Being honest about your planning and research process is a

You can help head off major problems by including your partner in your planning from the very start.

great way to bring them onboard and enable them to give you realistic encouragement. Of course, if you're in a relationship, your planning will affect the other person. You can help head off major problems by including your partner in your planning from the very start.

You will need to lead the process of setting expectations, sharing information, and shaping the understanding of your friends and family. Show them why your plan is best for everyone in the long run. Be willing to talk and share more than usual. Some people plan loudly or bounce ideas off others as a natural part of their process. Others bottle up everything inside until they figure it all out. Shoot for being somewhere in the middle, so you can bring the essential people in your life along with you step by step.

As with any major life change (e.g., marriage, parenting, or moving to a new location), your friendships and relationships will need to shift and adjust. Some friends may be able to make the transition with you while others may fade to the background. Well-meaning acquaintances will tell you what they know or have heard, but they might not have all the facts or fully understand your unique plan. Take what you can, educate them if they'll let you, and keep moving forward.

Have you been burned by people who overpromised and underdelivered? Planning is a great way to keep from making these mistakes for yourself. Don't focus solely on the high flyers and award winners in an industry. Instead, get an idea of what "average" looks like. Look for clues about the most common problems and setbacks, so you can have a plan in place to navigate them. Much industry research exists to help you find benchmarks and baselines, identify unmet needs, and look for ways to differentiate your business and disrupt the status quo.

Does it seem like your Facebook feed is full of other people talking about how they got where they wanted to be? Before you compare yourself to them or borrow their tactics, make sure to compare your original situation to theirs. Identify similarities before copying their methods.

Be intentional about putting your plan in place and choosing your support team. Your plan and your team will help you avoid being swept away with emotion either by dreams that might be a bit grandiose or by sudden feelings of overwhelm or despair. Highs and lows are a natural part of moving outside your comfort zone into new territory. You don't have to chart your course and travel the path alone.

As you plan, look for places where you are duplicating effort, missing opportunities, or feeling paralyzed by options. Can you see a way to simplify and put that extra time and energy toward something else? The goal of planning is to create ease and clarity around the steps required to make money, achieve abundance, and fulfill your dream. Planning helps to reduce resistance, so you can reach your goal with fewer obstacles and frustration.

Are you still reluctant when you think about planning? Maybe it will help to think about planning like a map or an itinerary for a road trip and not like a straitjacket. An itinerary can be changed and tweaked, helping you reach your destination and enjoy the journey. Give yourself permission to make some intentional "side trips." Attend a conference and allow yourself some extra time to be a tourist. Have fun while you're getting to know other business owners who are also starting out. Be serious about your planning, but leave room to relax and enjoy life along the way!

NEXT STEPS

1. Make a list of things you need to research to find out more about the new direction you want to take. Brainstorm as many ideas as you can.

2. Look at each item and think about how you could do the research. Don't stop with "look it up." Try to find a range of options (e.g., watching videos, attending conferences, visiting in person, taking knowledgeable people out to lunch, doing informational interviews, and getting hands-on practice). Now that you've considered multiple ways to learn, does it seem less daunting?

FOOD FOR THOUGHT

Do You Want a Hobby or a Business?

My client Mary resisted coming up with revenue projections. Not just three, four, or five years out, but even for year one. She said that she couldn't imagine doing the things necessary to attract clients and wondered aloud whether she even wanted to keep working.

"Maybe it's just a hobby," she said.

What pushed Mary into making up her mind? Business insurance. When she applied for insurance, she thought that she would need an annual revenue goal, and she came up with one. Something shifted at that point, and she decided that it was going to be a business and not a hobby. She set up the legal structure and bank account and is working on a plan. Now that she owns the fact that she is starting a business, her steps are intentional and not reactionary, and she is much more confident.

CHAPTER 7

Branding

Having a good idea is important. However, by itself, it's not a guarantee of success. Show your credibility and differentiate your business, products, and services from all the others in your field.

Sales vs. Marketing

What's the difference between "sales" and "marketing"? Do you have to learn how to do both to get your new business off the ground? What if you don't think you'll like selling or marketing? What if you don't think you'll be good at it?

While people often use the terms "sales" and "marketing" interchangeably, they have different meanings. For the purposes of this book, we'll use these two words as they relate to your planning process:

- "Sales" first identifies a potential customer and then continues through the transaction that puts your product(s) in the customer's hands. This process includes lead generation, managing and tracking leads, going to events where the emphasis is on transactions, and managing the art of closing the deal.

* "Marketing" is a plan that makes your product(s) and business known, liked, and desired by a prospective customer. This plan includes paid advertising, your website, your social-media outreach, public relations through articles or speaking engagements, your logo, your product packaging, your tagline, and everything else you do. The intended result is that your prospect recognizes your product, knows why they need it, and wants to find a way to buy it.

Marketing drives sales. If people don't know about your product(s) or service(s), or they don't understand why you are better than the competition, they won't be interested in buying from you. If you haven't thought about how to sell them the product(s) and make the money change hands, you won't stay in business and they won't get the help they need.

Sales is the fulfillment of marketing because, while marketing educates and builds the desire to purchase, sales completes the transaction and tracks the customer for future follow-up potential.

Where Branding Comes In

"Branding" means creating a unique look and position for your product, so the customer identifies those elements with your business—and only your business. Brands are around you every day (e.g., your favorite soda, the type of car you drive, the label in your shirt, and the manufacturer of your computer).

Big companies pour lots of money into branding because it creates customer preference. People want to buy a brand with which they've had good luck in the past or one that conveys status. Branding can simplify shopping for customers, eliminating the need to ponder 10 types of laundry detergent.

Brands can become so important that some people actually factor them into their identity. Have you ever heard someone say, "I'm an XYZ beer drinker" or "I only buy XYZ shampoo"? This behavior doesn't just occur while buying consumer products. Businesspeople buy from certain companies because they feel comfortable in knowing what to expect. The brand is well known, so their decision to purchase won't be scrutinized.

You don't have to have a big marketing budget to create your own brand. However, you do need to be intentional about it and realize that every decision you make—as well as every action—contributes to your brand.

> "Branding" means creating a unique look and position for your product, so the customer identifies those elements with your business—and only your business.

What is included in your brand? Almost everything you do.

Your business name and your logo are two of your biggest branding opportunities. The name(s) of your product(s) and the colors you use in packaging and materials and on your website are part of the mental image the prospect forms of you and your business. You want to be remembered positively and be distinct from the competition.

How should you name your company? Instead of trying to name your new business according to the products you sell, begin with your own name to give yourself greater scope. Realize that, as the head of your business, you are the embodiment of your brand. Some people take this to heart and choose a signature color to wear as an accent that ties into their logo or packaging. More importantly, every word you say, every email or social-media post you send, and every interaction you have with the people around you either strengthen or weaken your brand. It's a big responsibility.

Branding also includes your follow-up and your service as well as the quality and pricing of your products. Consistency is essential. You want your customers to be able to identify your business, so make sure that everything you create has the same "look," which reinforces your brand.

Logos and web design are two services essential to your brand, so don't try to cut corners. Use a professional with experience in branding, ask for references, check their portfolio, and be prepared to pay for good work. You want to do this right, so you don't have to redo it later. Since a good logo and website can last awhile, you want it to be the best.

How do you know what a good logo designer and website builder charges? Ask. Look at the materials of other professionals you meet and see whose logos and websites really stand out. Ask them who they worked with, and then check out the artist or web designer's site. Look for pricing information, and study samples of their work. If you haven't paid for these kinds of services before, you might discover that they cost more than you expected. That's because good work requires a professional with experience, and the outcome will represent you and your business for a long time.

Once you've done some research, come up with a budget and a plan for the items you'll need. Don't go for the quickest or the cheapest. This is one time that you want the best you can afford.

Most importantly, as you embody your brand, be yourself. Don't try to copy anyone else. Draw on your own personality, energy, and style. Have fun with it, but always remember that everything you do reflects on your business, so you want to be your best ambassador.

 **NEXT STEPS**

1. Think about your logo. Experiment with colors and fonts. Pay attention to the logos that are all around you. What do you like? Which ones don't grab you?

2. Look at the branding that your competitors in this new business are using. What are they doing well? What could be better?

FOOD FOR THOUGHT

Requesting Reviews, References, and Testimonials

Many people who have gotten over their initial reluctance about attracting clients and asking for the sale become suddenly shy when it comes to requesting reviews, references, and testimonials from satisfied customers.

Perhaps this reluctance originates from our parents, who told us not to "toot our own horn." This is outdated advice because, in today's social media-driven world, we have to be our own biggest cheerleader. While happy customers might love what you do, they're busy and often don't realize how important it is to post reviews for companies they want to see thrive.

Perhaps willing clients who want to write a review or testimonial don't know how to go about it. Help them overcome their nervousness and make sure they leave a recommendation that works hard for your business. Not all testimonials are created equal.

Think about the difference between these two examples:

1. "I love working with Mary. Her business helped me a lot."

   OR

2. "Mary changed the whole way I think about my business. She was always supportive, but she called me on it when I tried to do less than my best or stay in my comfort zone. Thanks to Mary, I feel prepared to create a hiring plan that will help me recruit the best talent while making sure my company meets all legal require-

ments. I'm looking forward to happier employees and less turnover!"

Which review would you rather have? Obviously, the second one. Why? It includes specific and special details about working with Mary, describes how she made a difference, and ends with a tangible, positive outcome. How do you get your customers to write great recommendations? You have to educate them.

You can create a recommendation request template like this:

Dear [name].

I've really enjoyed working with you, and I'm so excited about everything you've accomplished. Would you be willing to take a minute and write a recommendation for me on [location where you want the review posted, like LinkedIn, Google, Yelp, Facebook business page, or your website]?

Here are a couple of suggestions to keep in mind, so other people will get the most benefit out of what you write:

- Be specific about what problem(s) we tackled.

- Add details about what made our interaction particularly helpful to you.

- List tangible results and what they mean for you.

Thank you so much. I genuinely appreciate the chance to be of service to you, and I look forward to connecting with you again soon.

Be sure to get permission to use their name and company to attribute the quote because named references are much more powerful than anonymous ones or first-name attributions.

Does asking for that information feel uncomfortable to you? Remember: This client likes you and wants to help. They are perhaps unsure how to write a good recommendation. You're making it easier for them to help you by letting them know what you expect and guiding them through the process.

Regardless of where a customer leaves a recommendation, you can use their quote anywhere (e.g., your website's landing pages (single web pages that appear in response to clicking on a search result or an online advertisement), your newsletter, social-media pages, brochures, signage, trade-show graphics, and advertisements).

Don't be shy about making the most of good reviews and recommendations. They provide "social proof," which is reassurance that someone is doing the right thing because other people say they're doing the right thing. Testimonials and recommendations help overcome new customers' hesitance of working with an unknown quantity (you). The more references and recommendations you gather, the less you have to tell prospects how good you are because you now have other satisfied customers doing it for you!

Collecting referrals and testimonials is a never-ending process. It can be easy to let it slide when you're busy, but you want to have as many recommendations as you can from as wide a range of customers as possible. Keep them fresh and updated. If you don't ask for recommendations as part of wrapping up every sale, you'll find yourself with a bunch of 10-year-old testimonials that no longer accurately reflect your services.

Make asking for recommendations, reviews, and testimonials a habit!

CHAPTER 8

Pick a Business Model

You've thought about what kind of business you want to create. Have you also thought about what type of business model is best suited to your goals?

The structure of a business is a combination of what it needs to deliver its services/products and how it needs to be set up from a tax/accounting standpoint. This is a pretty deep topic, and this chapter raises the subject for further research and discussion with your CPA or attorney.

So Many Choices

- What do you want to achieve with this new business?

- Are you looking for a steady source of income? A retirement side gig? A part-time-for-now job you can gradually build into a full-time career?

- What size business do you have in mind?

- Are you happy dealing with customers one on one or working alone as a solopreneur?

- Do you envision your business growing to the point where you need a staff?
- Do you want to stay local or are you hungry to take your concept regional, national, or international?
- Can you provide your outcome anywhere (i.e., being location independent) or do you need to have a retail space, a manufacturing site, or an office?
- Do you want to remain fairly small, or do you secretly want to be the next big initial public offering on Wall Street?

Maybe it seems like some of these questions are putting the cart before the horse. Does it seem crazy to daydream about creating a business that gets gobbled up by investors for millions of dollars before you've even printed business cards?

On one hand, it may indeed seem crazy. There will be many decisions and hard work before you're ready to contemplate global domination. However, if you don't know what you ultimately want, you won't be able to chart a good path to get there. Knowing what you ultimately want will affect your choices all along the way. It's equally important to know what you don't want.

> Does it seem crazy to daydream about creating a business that gets gobbled up by investors for millions of dollars before you've even printed business cards?

Suppose you secretly want to create a business that is unique enough to eventually turn into a franchise, and then grow so big that an investor buys you out. That's quite different from someone who wants to slow down the pace after a career in a big corporation and do something hands on, individually focused, and maybe even artisanal.

Of course, there's no way to be certain that your big dream will actually happen. However, you can help those odds by building your business from the ground up to be capable of sustaining rapid growth. Or, for the person who wants slow and personal, make sure that a rush of success doesn't grow the business too far and too fast, with the result of sitting in a corner office and running the corporation you never wanted.

Before you apply for your business license or file "doing business as" (DBA) paperwork, decide whether you want to set up shop as a sole proprietorship, a professional partnership, a limited liability corporation, a personal assistant, an S Corporation, or any of the other variations. Each designation has benefits and liabilities, and it can be difficult (or expensive) to change your business structure later on. Get help from a knowledgeable professional (e.g., a CPA and/or a lawyer familiar with business law). This is something basic and important that you want to do right the first time.

Know Your Customers

We talked earlier about recognizing your customers and planning where to find them. For your business model, be clear about whom you serve, so you can plan a structure that delivers your product(s) in the best way.

Do you serve other businesses (e.g., document-shredding companies, business law firms, commercial cleaning services, or corporate security providers), or do you serve the public (e.g., restaurants; retail stores; medical providers; travel and entertainment firms; and artists, writers, and musicians, who create products that can be used by an individual rather than by a business)?

You'll hear the phrases "B2B" (also known as "business-to-business" or "B-to-B") or "B2C" (also known as "business-to-consumer" or "B-to-C"). Your choice between serving customers or other businesses will have a big impact on your branding, marketing, sales, and delivery methods.

If you choose B2B, you'll focus on industry trade shows, networking with corporate buyers, and government contracts, but your firm will be virtually invisible to regular consumers. Knowledge work, such as coaching and consulting, falls under B2B if the topic is business related, so you'll be tuned into networking opportunities that bring you into contact with businesspeople who need your expertise.

On the other hand, if you choose B2C, you might be selling directly to online consumers, looking to have your products picked up by a retail-store chain or to open your own store. You may be attending or have a booth at seasonal or specialty exhibitions that cater to the public. You'll be in a completely different world from your B2B counterparts.

Your choice of customer base also affects your pricing model, which is part of your business model and plan. This model is part of your sales planning, which has an impact on your brand and your marketing.

- Are you in the kind of business that gets new customers with free samples or free trials?
- Do people buy for themselves or for their business?
- Is it an individual purchase or a subscription?
- Do people need a membership to buy?
- Are you planning to create a community around your product(s) or service(s)?

These are important considerations. They'll have an impact on how you set up your website, what kind of software you'll need to handle and track sales, and how you need to brand and position your business.

Where Will You Work?

Where you plan to do your work has an impact on how you set up your business model. Many kinds of knowledge work can be done from a home office. Even jobs that require meeting with other professionals and clients can often be done from home by arranging to meet at coffee shops, rented presentation/meeting spaces, or other kinds of coworking/shared places.

Just because you need part-time or full-time helpers, you might be able to work from home if your team is virtual, meaning that you collaborate via the internet. Using virtual workers helps keep your costs low while offering flexible lifestyle choices to employees and saving them the cost and hassle of commuting. Keeping your team virtual and using independent contractors can enable you to bring workers in and out as demand rises or falls. This arrangement also allows for dynamic staffing to let you match skills to the project.

> **Keeping your team virtual and using independent contractors can enable you to bring workers in and out as demand rises or falls.**

Production, retail, or manufacturing space can often be contracted or shared instead of being rented or purchased outright, depending on your volume and specific needs. Investigate your options before you commit to a contract.

Defining your new business dream is an essential part of setting up the right business model to help you achieve your goals. It's worth a little planning up front to avoid expensive and time-consuming mistakes and create a business model that will make it easier for you to get where you want to go.

 **NEXT STEPS**

1. Take time to daydream your ideal end game. Do you want to own a huge corporation? Sell out to Wall Street? Build a franchise? Or do you want to do something intensely local and hands on? Write down your thoughts.

2. Read about the different types of business structures. Which one sounds best suited to what you want to build? If you've gotten to know other people who have the kind of business you want to create, ask them what structure they've chosen and why.

CHAPTER 9

Create Your Business Strategy Goals

D oes your head feel stuffed full of great ideas and questions? Are you having trouble getting your arms around what to do first? Now that you've done a lot of thinking, strategizing, and brainstorming, it's time to wrangle those wild ideas into priority order.

Roadmaps vs. Strategies

To avoid confusion, I'm going to use the term "roadmap" to talk about the detailed overview of what needs to be done in what order to achieve your goals. By doing this, we can save the term "business plan" for the combination of your roadmap and your strategies—the whole enchilada. Likewise, while goals can be big (e.g., starting a company) or small (e.g., printing business cards), I'm going to use the term "goal" for the larger vision and "milestones" for the smaller steps.

Here's the plan:

- Create a list of your priorities, listing them in the order of their importance.
- Focus on getting the top four priorities done in the first year. That's it. Just four. Feel better already?
- Break down what needs to get done quarterly, monthly, and weekly—even daily, if you want. This helps incorporate your top priorities into your daily life.

A good roadmap will help you waste less time, money, and energy. With a roadmap in place, you'll feel more satisfied because you will see outcomes faster. A roadmap takes away clutter and overwhelm. It enables you to stay fixed on your target, like a heat-seeking missile.

Your priorities list is a fluid and changeable document. You will constantly update and tweak it as business conditions change.

You have completed several big steps to get to this point! Now that you've set the strategy, you've thought about how to execute it and created specific milestones and tasks. What was huge and unruly is now smaller and doable.

How does a roadmap differ from a strategy?

- A "roadmap" is the overview of the route.
- A "strategy" contains the big building blocks, and the milestones are the bricks. A strategy might be for a year while the milestones can be shorter term (e.g., quarterly, monthly, weekly, or daily).

Your big goal is the master vision. Your roadmap is the sequence of key events that needs to occur (your strategy) to make that goal a reality. Milestones are the essential actions that create those individual key events.

For example:

- Your goal is to start a business.

- Your roadmap will likely contain key strategies like "build my network," "set up my business systems," and "determine my business structure."

- Your milestones to make these things happen might be things like "make a short list of networking groups to try and attend an event for each," "identify good information technology and HR partners," and "talk with a business attorney and CPA about business-structure alternatives."

Your roadmap, strategies, and milestones make up your plan and service your goals.

Creating a high-level strategy lets you know where you're going in the long term. As you do your milestone-setting, you can include the tools that will lay a strong foundation for your future.

A good roadmap will help you waste less time, money, and energy.

For example, if part of your strategy includes being a speaker to audiences of your potential customers:

- Your milestone-setting would incorporate how often you wanted to speak and to whom.

- Your tools might include email newsletter software and social-media sites, which help you build your platform. You'd know from the beginning that the tools should be an important part of your foundation and not a late addition.

- You would build a sales funnel, which is part of your marketing effort.

Here's where your past work experience can help or hinder you. If your previous roles were in management, you may have had a taste of top-down planning and seen how the contributions of individual people, departments, and even locations became part of the big picture. However, if you have only experienced bottom-up goals, you may not have had the chance to see how they factored into the final results. Was your annual review based on your individual tasks or how those outcomes impacted the overall company? In starting your own business, you will be wearing both hats (i.e., as the CEO and the individual contributor).

A good roadmap includes time management, so you aren't trying to do too much all at once. Think about it as setting up mile markers along the route to your final destination. When a milestone seems too large, look for ways to break it into smaller component tasks.

On the other hand, a roadmap keeps you focused on your destination, so you don't get distracted by the tourist traps along the highway. Be sure to consider cyclicality because some seasons may be naturally busier than others due to holidays and business cycles.

When to Ask for Help

People usually have two reactions when they get to the "milestones" step. They may feel overwhelmed because they aren't organized enough to prioritize. Or they understand the necessary critical path to put the required items in the order in which they can get done. Don't worry. Everyone starts out in the first group and can get to the second group by spending some time thinking about what steps are required.

Don't get bogged down in the process of prioritizing. Keep your focus on the outcome, on whom you serve, and on what change you want to see in the world. If you're having difficulty, it's okay to ask for help. Getting help from someone who is farther along in the process is perfectly fine. Asking for help doesn't mean that you're not smart enough to figure something out. It means that you know how to wisely use your time and connections to keep from spinning your wheels!

For people who are experts in their field or subject matter, it can be difficult to admit that they can use a hand while getting things organized. Please ask for help sooner rather than later. Don't wait until you're drowning! Make sure that you get a qualified coach or consultant. This is not the time to pick the cheapest option or to select the first name that comes up without carefully checking their qualifications.

If you're used to being in charge, getting help from a coach or consultant might require a shift in your personal approach. Be willing to listen to suggestions, adapt your behavior, and be **Don't get bogged down in the process of prioritizing.** receptive to new ideas or ways of approaching situations. You might discover that, due to a market shift that occurred as you were making your plans, you'll need to adjust. Better to find out this reality early and make the necessary changes than to find yourself farther down the road and run into real problems.

 **NEXT STEPS**

1. Grab a piece of paper and write down your goals, roadmap, strategies, and milestones. Don't worry if you have some blank spots. Do the levels nest like an outline? If it's messy, think about your priorities to help you get the pieces in the right place.

2. When you are thinking about big goals, keep your lifestyle, relationships, and health in mind and not just your business. Ideally, the overall plan you create for your business should serve all your life goals.

CHAPTER 10

Sustain and Monitor

As you build your new business, how will you keep your name in the community and remain current as you figure out your behind-the-scenes issues? How will you gather and track the necessary data to judge how all the aspects of your plan are delivering on their expected outcomes?

Tracking is essential to know which efforts and investments are paying off and where you can shift your time and money to greater advantage. As you read this book, think about what activities you can monitor to achieve better analyses and decision-making results.

Stay Mission Driven

Always keep the impact you want to make in the world central in your planning. That's your mission, and it's what you ultimately want to achieve: the transformation you bring to your customers and your industry. As daily issues and distractions nip at your heels, it can be easy to focus on mundane tasks and lose sight of the main goal. The trick is to handle the small stuff and never lose sight of your ultimate mission, which requires constant self-checking and refocusing your priorities. You're playing a long game. You are looking to build relationships that will sustain your shift from employee to business owner. Some people may help you right now, some will become constant partners, and others are resources that you cultivate for the future.

Part of building a business is building and sustaining connections with people. Not just potential customers, but referral sources, mentors, vendors/suppliers, and "helpful others." Those "helpful others" are people who are in positions to make your life easier if they have and keep a positive impression of you. They can be leaders within your industry, officials or regulators, outside observers (e.g., journalists and reviewers), and physical neighbors to your business or the people at the forefront of causes that matter to your clientele.

Sustaining your business requires maintaining relationships as well as keeping an eye on the bottom line. If you're naturally a social person, you might find relationship-building easy and the metrics part less natural. If your default is about numbers and spread-

Part of building a business is building and sustaining connections with people.

sheets, you might have to work up some courage to get out there and make connections. A good business strategy requires some of both.

Sustaining relationships means that you have to see what you can give, not just what you can get. When you stay in touch, it's not just about your needs. Find out how you can help, even if there's no immediate (or potential) way the person can pay you back. Give first because it's the right thing to do. You're building goodwill and letting people see your character. Keep track of the people you meet, keep building your list, and use your existing network to get feedback. Look for ways to stay in regular contact, so you can nurture the relationships that will help you achieve your goal.

Become Data Driven

Part of the formula for success lies in continually working *on* your business as well as *in* it. Gathering and using data to refine your tactics are key secrets to success. Gather data first. It's amazing how many business owners don't track vital information beyond sales numbers.

Here are some important data elements to add to the list:

- New clients acquired by time period (e.g., week, month, quarter, or year)

- Price point at which sales occurred

- Percentage of revenue contributed by each product/service offering

- Sources of new clients

- Sales to repeat customers

- Sales spikes after speaking engagements, trade shows, and other events

- Conversion rate, including the number of prospects that turn into sales

- Feedback from customers, including their likes and dislikes, what they want to see more or less of, and their unfulfilled needs

Now that I've gotten you started, can you think of more things that could be useful to know?

Having this information helps you determine what delivers your best results in getting new clients and what kinds of offers work well at bringing in new or additional orders. This will help you set or adjust your revenue targets and your goal for new customers every month. You'll be able to see which products/services need to grow, which aren't profitable, and which might need more promotion.

Looking for a spike after an event can help you budget your time, money, and travel more wisely. Not all sales happen on the show floor or in the back of the room. Sometimes people need to go home and think about it, wait for the next paycheck or budget adjustment, or get approval (depending on the type/ price of the product). An event where you didn't close a lot of deals at the show might still be profitable if you can link it to a bump in sales after the fact.

Many business owners overlook feedback as a form of valuable data. Ask your customers what you're doing right and where you can improve. Then act on the suggestions that align with your plan. Find out what they think are your strongest benefits and your real appeal. You might be amazed to find out that it's different than what you believe. Feedback also helps you stop doing what doesn't work sooner rather than later, so you are putting your energy in the right places. Success requires constant refining, and feedback is an essential part of that process.

Rethink Your Pricing to Sustain Your Growth

Revisit your business-model pricing decisions as you think about sustaining and monitoring. If you're giving away something, how many people are accepting the gift? Are you getting contact information in exchange for the freebie? If so, can you use those email addresses to track how much paid business the freebie generated? Did people who took the freebie also buy other products or services? Ask for more information? Attend an event? Ultimately, your freebies need to generate sales, or they aren't worth your energy.

If you're doing one-on-one programs, is your capacity filling up to the point where you might be well served by offering group programs? Group programs let you serve more people, albeit usually at a slightly lower price point than individual work. This broadens your number of potential customers and gives you the chance to sell group participants into an advanced one-on-one package or mastermind program (applying the sales-funnel concept again).

Has the number of customers reached the point where it might make sense to offer a subscription or membership? These offerings are great for businesses with recurring new releases or products that are frequently either reordered or purchased together with other products. The benefit to you is that customers who subscribe/belong never miss a new release or forget to reorder.

> **Group programs let you serve more people, albeit usually at a slightly lower price point than individual work.**

Can you transform your audience/customer base into a community? This might be a Facebook group, a series of recurring live events, a special and exclusive newsletter, or all of the above. A community increases your involvement with your base. It encourages your base to become energized by getting to know each other and sharing tips, helping each other, talking about what the product/service has done for them, and essentially cementing their postpurchase satisfaction.

By reevaluating your pricing models, you can see which areas are growing and which might need more attention. You can gauge where you're approaching capacity and anticipate demand by creating new services/programs to address those needs. Most importantly, you retain flexibility and scalability, so you can adapt to the needs of your consumers and to shifts in the marketplace. When you collect and track data, you'll find opportunities and avoid unpleasant surprises.

Since we're talking about sustaining and monitoring, let's discuss how to get from a community to a mastermind group, which is a long-term growth strategy toward which many businesses build. Have you heard about mastermind groups? Do you wonder what all the fuss is about? We have talked about the definition of a community, and a mastermind group is a specialized type of community. In an expert-centric community, your members are drawn to share an ongoing conversation with you or your firm, so that they never miss any crucial information and are always informed. They also get to know each other to trade proven tweaks and ideas and share resources, but it's all focused on the products/services you offer.

A mastermind group is a small, carefully chosen, confidential group of rising-star, subject-matter experts. Each member has a different specialty from a unique industry (to avoid competition in the group), sharing their expertise to solve individual business challenges. The founder is the leader, but the group members mentor each other. This setup requires building trust and developing a high comfort level. These groups can be a powerful way to offer added value for the "stars" that come out of your community.

Members within a mastermind group use each other like an informal board of directors.

Mastermind groups enable you to go deeper than coaching. They can include exclusive live and online events, teaching modules, specialized education, and one-on-one personal time. Whether you join someone else's mastermind group or start your own, they can be valuable ways to scale your business more quickly.

Members within a mastermind group use each other like an informal board of directors. They become a sounding board for each other and offer advice, referrals, and recommendations based on similar work experiences. Collaborative opportunities often arise out of the complimentary types of expertise represented in the group.

Good mastermind groups provide accountability, making sure that members act on what they've learned to keep making progress. Be sure to select members based on their ability to play well with others, to be supportive instead of competitive, to share information instead of hoarding it, and to have the personalities necessary to get along and engender trust.

Reevaluate Your Networking Return on Investment

While we're on the topic of communities, let's continue our discussion about networking. When you find the right networking groups, they become supportive and valuable communities in which you can gain influence and credibility, meet resources and collaborative partners, learn, and give back. The wrong groups can waste your time, drain your energy (and wallet), and leave you disillusioned and disappointed. Let's see how applying metrics to networking can help you save time, effort, and money while boosting your results.

How do you choose the right groups? How does that choice change as your business matures?

Decide what you want out of a networking group and understand what you have to give to it. This will change as your business matures. At first, you'll be looking for referrals, new clients, and resources. Although these components will always exist, as you grow, you will be looking for collaborative partners, higher-level resources, and referrals to larger or different kinds of prospects. Some groups will grow with you and some will need to be left behind (unless you're in a mentor role) as your needs change.

Size up the membership of any group you are considering:

- Are they all at your current level of expertise?

- Is there a range of business maturity from start-up to thriving middle to large?

- Are companies at all levels represented in the leadership and focus of programming, or does it slant in favor of one at the expense of others? For example, is it all about start-ups but not much about addressing the needs of established businesses?

- Do the big companies dominate?
- Does the membership represent your target market?
- How many of your competitors are present and are they entrenched (e.g., in leadership roles and sponsorships)?

You're not being snobby; you're being smart. You want to make sure that there will be a payoff for the time and energy you invest because you can only give so much of yourself. If you're active in this group, you can't be as active elsewhere. Make your tradeoffs wisely.

Does the audience in the networking group know that they need your expertise? Just because they need you and your expertise doesn't mean that they understand the benefits you offer. You can educate them about those benefits to a point. However, sometimes their learning curve is too big or they're not really interested in changing, so you have to walk away and find a more receptive group.

Does the group's membership heavily represent a particular industry? For example, many networking groups cater to real-estate professionals and the companies that provide related services (e.g., remodelers, appraisers, banks, and home inspectors). Other groups lean toward multilevel-marketing owners. These types of businesspeople might benefit from what you're offering, but they may not be open to adding your services or going beyond what is provided in their industry education programs. If you find yourself boxed out, go elsewhere.

Consider a group's branding. Are they involved in community projects? Do they run local, state, or national charity events? Are they known for offering quality educational programs (i.e., ones you can sponsor, speak at, or learn from)? Do they have a good reputation? Some groups have well-known brands (e.g., Chamber of Commerce, Kiwanis, Rotary Club,

Optimists, and Toastmasters). The personality of the local chapter can vary tremendously, so explore them if you're interested. Don't feel obligated to belong and move on if the chapter isn't a good fit.

Where do you find networking groups? Word of mouth is always good. You can find them on Meetup.com, in the calendar section of your local business paper, on online community bulletin boards, and as part of state or national professional or industry organizations. Don't forget to look at groups that serve particular constituencies, including minority business owners, women, and LGBTQA professionals.

Whatever groups you join, create metrics to determine your return on investment. Give yourself six months to a year to become established and let people get to know you. Be visible by offering to volunteer, speak, sponsor, or provide resources. Then monitor the value. Are you getting new clients? Are you meeting people who have helped you find new resources, partnerships, or opportunities that you wouldn't have otherwise had? Has it opened doors for you?

Where do you find networking groups?

On the other hand, if you take stock and realize that you're doing all the giving and not seeing opportunities arise in return, it's time to reevaluate. Unless you've specifically chosen to invest in a group as a charitable or giving-back endeavor, there should be benefit to you and to them. Maybe you're in the wrong group. Perhaps the group isn't philosophically inclined to help all members grow or there's a clique getting in the way. Whatever it is, use your scarce time and energy to better advantage by knowing when to cut ties and move on.

Nurture Your Relationships

I've talked before about working *on* your business and not just working *in* it. That means creating and nurturing your personal relationships and making sure that you give them their due.

As you network, you'll meet a lot of people. Some of those folks will eventually turn into customers. Tracking when/ whether your contacts become clients is called your "conversion rate." This rate will show how many people, on average, you have to meet to get one new client. It will likely vary by product/service. Look at the overall numbers as well as by specific offering, so you understand how many prospective connections you'll need to yield one new customer.

If you're coming from a corporate sales background, this concept isn't new to you. People with other areas of expertise will be wading in for the first time. Converting prospects to customers is a skill, and it can be learned. Some people do it naturally while others have to acquire the techniques. If you were the kid who could talk anyone into anything, you're probably a natural. Everyone else has to learn and practice. Books and training programs can help once you know that your conversion rate is important.

What does your conversion rate tell you? Plenty! Ideally, you want to know your conversion rate to keep your "pipeline" full and be able to roughly predict future income. Your pipeline is the influx of new contacts and relationships that you are nurturing to turn prospects into customers.

For example:

- On average, let's say that you can convert 50 percent of prospects into buying a particular product over a three-month period. Once you know this statistic, you can create an income estimate based on those sales.

- If you increase your conversion rate by 15 percent, it translates into a "raise" of the same amount in new income.

- If you convert a higher percentage of prospects, you'll earn more money with less effort because you won't need to bring in a huge number of new contacts to hit your income projections.

Your pipeline is important for more than just new clients. You should also have pipelines for potential collaborative partners, possible corporate sponsors, speaking opportunities, and leadership roles.

Your roadmap, milestones, and monitoring skills all come into play here. If you know that, in two years, your roadmap includes a milestone of giving a certain number of speeches, then start identifying organizations and opportunities now to warm them up. Contact the groups, get to know their members and leaders, make yourself a valuable booster and resource, and let them get to know you and your expertise.

Stay in touch with contacts to nurture future connections. Keep track of the people you meet who have promising potential and look for ways to help them achieve their goals. Find ways to

What does your conversion rate tell you?

maintain regular contact, so the connection doesn't grow cold. These contacts can be through online programs like LinkedIn, via live events, or through membership in organizations. Developing these connections takes time, but it is valuable to both parties in the long run and well worth the effort.

Don't write off someone just because it's not the right time to work together. Their needs and situations will change, and so will yours. Keep track of the people you meet because you never know when you will suddenly need someone or something. A person who didn't seem to fit your plan at one time may suddenly become the missing piece of the puzzle.

Survey your pool of contacts on ideas you're considering, market trends, or the impact of real-world events on your industry. Asking for their input/opinions makes them feel valued and keeps them involved in your growth. Periodically, take someone knowledgeable to lunch and interview them to learn more about their perspective. You'll uncover valuable gems and deepen your relationships.

It takes time to build relationships and for a mutually beneficial opportunity to arise. If you can bring good value, then you are doing them as much of a favor as they are doing for you. Approach these relationships as a win-win solution. Build relationships that will sustain you as a person and as a business over the long run.

What about outside of work? Be sure to pay attention and nurture your personal relationships and self-care just as avidly as you do your professional roles. It's easy to get lost in the excitement (and work) of building a business, neglecting time for friends, family, and yourself. Make an appointment to clear calendar time for your partner, extended family, children, and friends. Pencil in appointments for self-care (e.g., getting a massage, going to the gym, doing a yoga class, or taking a vacation).

> **Survey your pool of contacts on ideas you're considering, market trends, or the impact of real-world events on your industry.**

Make time in your schedule to run your business and handle administrative tasks (e.g., billing and preparing taxes). This time includes reviewing data and metrics that you collect to see how your pipeline is working, comparing protected income to actual income, monitoring your conversion rate, and seeing which products/services are selling well and which need a boost. You don't want to watch your metrics every minute, but reviewing them once a week and definitely once a month is like taking the temperature of your business.

Set Boundaries and Expectations

Starting and running a business isn't a 9-to-5 job, but it shouldn't burn you out. Set boundaries to stay balanced. "Boundaries" are a separation between one role and another or parameters you set about what you will and won't accept. Depending on your prior workplaces, you may not have experience with good boundary-setting.

Creating boundaries can mean:

- Setting aside one day a week to spend with family or just relax

- Refusing to work over a certain number of hours a week, even if it requires you to slow down the growth of your business or hire help

- Creating clear expectations and terms, and then managing reality to comply with those expectations

- Requiring a commitment on your part that your boundaries won't suddenly be cast aside every time there is an "emergency"

Modern corporate life can be all-consuming, especially if you worked 80-hour weeks, had travel that obliterated your free time, or had a boss who phoned, emailed, or texted you at all hours and expected you to reply. This is your chance to fix these situations and create a healthier, happier life. You can work hard, but take time to nurture the other parts of your life. Relationships wither without constant tending, and good balance increases the odds that you will feel successful in both your business and personal lives.

Investing time into your self-care and into nurturing your friends and family helps you be more resilient. Resilience is a key trait for successful businesspeople because the world is constantly changing. You have to learn, grow, experiment, and regroup to stay in the game. Having a solid support team outside of work and putting time into your relationships and well-ness keep you strong enough to handle the challenges.

Over time, your business will be like a continuous wave with peaks and valleys. You'll start up and then fly! Then there will be a change that requires you to shift/pivot. Then you'll start up again and fly. Then you'll repeat the cycle all over again. These shift/pivot moments aren't failures. They describe how the business reality works: a cycle of continual and constant reinvention. That's why your plan can never be final and immutable because it needs to continually evolve to respond to changes in the market and to your customers.

Don't base your expectations on your parents' business experiences.

Don't base your expectations on your parents' business experiences. That's the unquestioned default for many of us because that's what we learned growing up. We internalized their expectations without realizing it. The world is a different place now. Business at all levels is less stable. Nothing remains the same for long. Everything is in constant flux. In many cases, we don't have the institutional or social safety nets on which our parents could rely. When you realize that you might be clinging to outdated expectations, you can free yourself and deal with the current world to make new plans.

NEXT STEPS

1. Think about the concept of boundaries. Where have you had difficulty setting or maintaining boundaries in the past? What steps could you take to keep that from happening again? Are there boundaries you haven't set in the past but need to set now in order to achieve your goals and best life?

2. Make a list of the assumptions and expectations you have about how business works, what success means, how successful people act, and how life is supposed to unfold for middle age and onward. Now look at your list. Have you absorbed assumptions from cultural expectations, your parents' experiences, or the media without questioning whether or not those ideas are current and valid? Make up a list of how you want to answer instead of how you think you should answer, and then compare them.

CHAPTER 11

Evaluate and Modify

You've got your business roadmap, your strategies, and your milestones in place. Your fledgling business is getting off the ground. Clients are lining up, and real money is coming in. As tempting as it can be to think that you're in the home stretch, the truth is that it's time to reflect on how things are going, so you can evaluate the results and modify your approach where needed.

Constant Tweaking Is the Secret to Success

Why do you need to bother evaluating your business when things are going well? If things aren't moving along as you planned, why take time away from your crisis management to evaluate your situation? In both cases, it's because a little evaluation now can save you a whole lot of wheel-spinning later.

When something isn't working, change it sooner rather than later and save yourself a lot of grief. As you think about how your new business is taking shape, think about where things are going smoothly. Double check to assure that there isn't a looming bump in the road to derail that success.

For example, is your business scalable and able to grow eas-
ily as new clients come in? Or will you have to change suppli-
ers, facilities, or delivery mechanisms and add staff at a certain
point of increased demand? If you can see a pinch point coming, jump ahead of the curve and plan to make that transition
as smooth as possible, so it doesn't take you by surprise and
potentially disappoint your customers.

Even with your roadmap in place, circumstances will surprise
you. Approach surprises with the three Rs: review, research, and
revise:

- **Review** what's going on.

- **Research** the rough spots as you stop to take a closer
  look.

- **Revise** small problems before they become big ones and
  big problems before they become huge.

Try to avoid jumping to a conclusion about the right correc-
tive action to take in a situation. You might not have all the
information yet to make that decision. Slow down and do some
research to make sure that you thoroughly understand the
nature of the problem and what your options are. Then revise
your approach and move on.

The review-research-revise cycle is an ongoing part of management—sometimes on a daily basis. Think of your business
like you do your car. Your car might be running well, but it
won't keep working at top efficiency if you skip oil changes,
tire checks, and other regular diagnostics. Your business is the
same. It's much better to recognize a problem in your business
before it happens and fix it instead of letting the issue upset
your progress.

Modify Your Mindset

Evaluating your mindset can be the most difficult part of the process because it requires thinking about how you think. We often get comfortable with our familiar ways of seeing the world and coming to conclusions. However, we don't usually think about how we work out the logic of those decisions (and perhaps miss options and opportunities along the way) until something shakes us up.

The first mental adjustment to make is realizing that, no matter how much you plan, how good your research is, or how talented you are, things won't be perfect from day one. Even with all your life experiences and skills, you'll feel insecure and go through a learning curve that takes you out of your comfort zone. It took time to become proficient at what you used to do, and it will require time to get good at your new work. Take a few deep breaths and give yourself permission to learn and make mistakes.

> **Evaluating your mindset can be the most difficult part of the process because it requires thinking about how you think.**

Making mental adjustments is part of the process of seeking mastery, which is an ongoing part of life. It's okay to ask for help along the way. The approaches and solutions that worked for you in other situations and settings might not work for you now, so ask for input and advice from your mentors, peers, teams, coaches, or consultants. Asking for help means that you are growing. It's a strength, not a weakness. If you had jumped to work at another company instead of starting your own business, you would need time to settle in. That's exactly what you're doing with the business you've started. It's normal and part of the process.

Surviving and thriving corporations constantly adapt to remain relevant and change with the needs of their customers. If that kind of forward-thinking wasn't part of your prior experiences, it is a good time to read about best practices of firms that are leading their industries and innovating successfully. You might be a small business and they might be giants, but you can still learn a lot of new approaches and ways of thinking to adapt to your situation.

Don't be afraid to admit when you don't know something. Instead, seek out someone who can teach you or find a way to learn. Ego is a huge obstacle, but people who can't admit that they need help often stall out because they can't do it by themselves. Be open to learning, and make it a habit to ask plenty of questions.

Momentum can be a trap. Have you ever rolled something heavy and then tried to change its course? Once something gets moving, changing direction can be difficult. The same is true for psychology as well as physics. Maybe you've invested a lot of time in a strategy and the market changes. It's tempting to stay the course. However, if the market has shifted, holding onto an old roadmap won't help.

Don't be afraid to admit when you don't know something.

Discover that "failure" isn't a dirty word. People who aren't willing to fail aren't willing to try because trying doesn't guarantee success. In fact, people who have the most success also have the most failure because they are continually trying out new approaches and discarding the ones that don't work. Celebrate the times when you took a risk and it didn't work out because you've hopefully learned something that will increase your chances of success the next time. Stop, evaluate, and pivot when necessary, which are essential actions for success.

Create an environment where the people around you are willing to innovate because they know that experimentation—and the inevitable failures—won't be held against them. Companies stagnate when they are too afraid to risk making a mistake and stick to doing things the way they've always done them. *That* is a real recipe for failure!

Think about mental shifts in the same way you alter your route around road construction. No matter how much you want to stick to your original itinerary, there's no way to argue when a bridge is out. The key to success is keeping your ultimate destination in mind even when the route changes.

Do not become emotionally tied to a particular approach or a specific outcome. The route changes. Sometimes you'll end up in a place that you didn't expect. Be open to opportunity and you might find that your detour took you to a better destination than the one you originally planned.

NEXT STEPS

1. Think about times when something didn't go as planned or didn't work out on the first try (e.g., a dinner reservation, a vacation itinerary, a remodeling project, or something business related). This can include anything that "failed." What happened instead? Did you find something better and unexpected? Were you open to enjoying the new opportunity or upset about the failure?

2. Take some quiet time and think about how you were raised to see and define "failure." For some people, failure is about competition, not just results (e.g., not just earning an "A" but also having the highest grade in the class). For others, anything less than perfection was not good enough. Some people were trained to associate failure with shame, disappointment, and worthlessness. Now is the time to get rid of old, toxic ideas in order to free yourself to experiment and fly!

CHAPTER 12

Put It All Together and Get Started!

At the beginning of the book, you were asked a series of questions. I would like to revisit those questions again, so that you can look at them through a more informed lens. I invite you to take some time and really consider each of the following questions again:

- Have you been thinking about starting your own business?

- Are you considering a big shift in your career path?

- Are you leaving your job (e.g., retiring or downsizing) and thinking of a move into entrepreneurship?

- Do you want to leave your job but aren't sure how to create a better one?

- Are you looking for an active retirement that allows you to keep your hand in the game?

- Are you an early-stage entrepreneur who is considering pivoting in a new direction?

If you are here, now, chances are that you fit into one of the above categories. What are you waiting for? This book will help you create an action plan that will minimize lost time and dead ends while enabling you to get off to the best possible start and increase your satisfaction, and your success.

It's time to get started!

Bonus Checklist

Chapter 1: Get Started

- Consider your options before proceeding. Pause and cover all the bases.

- What do you love/hate to do? Don't recreate the bad parts of what came before.

- Align what you value in your life and in your business.

- Come up with your "what you do" concept that hooks into your passion.

- Go into your new business strong by thinking through your options. Be resilient, empowered, and confident.

- Get yourself onboard with your program by confronting unconscious bias about self-employment.

- Realize that part of getting started is building a team, so start looking for allies.

- Focus on what you want to do in retirement now. Start living on your retirement budget to see how well you've estimated.

- Get out of the habit of referring to what you do with a title instead of with an outcome.

Chapter 2: Pause-Reflect-Reset

- Create your plan before you dive in. Act from intention, not reaction. Project where you want to be one, three, and five years from now.

- A good idea isn't enough. Create a "10,000-foot overview" of where you see yourself going.

- Realize that starting a business is a major life transition.

- Recognize that you need to grieve and let go of your old life and expectations.

- Take a look at the big picture. In what industry will your new business be? Where do you fit with what's already there? Do you differentiate or disrupt? Is it saturated or is there room to grow?

- Plan to take care of yourself. A major shift creates shock. Prepare for friendship changes, find new groups, explore networking options, and weed out time-wasters and groups that are a bad fit.

- Look at your transferable skills, play to your strengths, and figure out how to demonstrate what you have to offer.

- What is your brand? How can you evolve into new skills?

- Plan now to deal with a crisis of confidence when the shock wears off.

- PAUSE. Think about your strengths and define them (tangible/intangible and not just what you learned in school). Factor in different types of intelligence. If you're not sure, ask people who know you well. Old strengths might need to be fine-tuned for new situations.

Chapter 3: Stay Focused

- Be mindful of working *in* your business or *on* your business. Look for ways to find a balance.
- It doesn't have to be perfect! Watch out for perfectionism, and don't get caught up in minutiae.
- This is the first time to think about who *you* are and what *you* want. Learn how to be okay with being a work in progress. Be ready to pivot and evolve past your comfort zone.
- Get past your fear of failure, or at least don't let it hold you back.
- Remember that you are not alone.

Chapter 4: Set Priorities

- With so many possibilities, you will need to prioritize, so always come back to your plan.
- Do research on your industry, your market, your potential customer base, your product, your competitors, your pricing, and the differentiation between your business and others in the same industry.
- Look at your values in life and align them with your business values.
- Think about your marketing plan and determine the tools and skills you'll need.
- Get the fundamentals straight. Learn about taxes, including withholding taxes for employees, hiring practices, intellectual property protection, and steps needed to obtain a business license.
- Create teams, including peers, a CPA, an attorney, a coach/mentor, financial/legal experts, and wellness professionals.

- Look at your revenue stream. Determine what you will need to cover expenses and your long-term goals for retirement.
- Factor in health insurance. Think about potential difficulties and options for getting credit.
- Look ahead to estate and succession planning.
- Keep your overhead low. Decide whether you can work from home or if you need an "office" to meet clients.
- Think about how you will introduce yourself when you run into former colleagues/vendors/customers. Reposition yourself, and don't use a title as a label. Focus on what you do and the outcomes you create, not your title. Expect initial discomfort and understand how you can reposition former colleagues as allies, resources, and customers.
- Remember that where you start is not where you end up.
- Strive for balance but realize that you are always dialing effort and energy up and down.
- Consider the stress that you will experience if you don't talk about your plans with your partner. Explore expectations, assumptions, priorities, and potential relationship impact.
- Don't be afraid to ask for help before things get out of control. Try to be proactive instead of reactive.
- Plan so that your team and resources evolve as your business does.
- Resilience is stronger with a good foundation, so analyze what skills you need and how to acquire them.

Chapter 5: Evaluate Options

- Determine why you are thinking about starting your own business. Understand how your circumstances (e.g., downsizing, retiring, getting a windfall, and experiencing life changes) have influenced the choices you are considering.

- Fully consider whether to jump into your new business full time or start with a side gig.

- Consider the pros/cons to doing a part-time ramp up.

- Maintain your current job to cover expenses.

- Build up your clientele, gain new skills, put the pieces in place, get training/certification, network, and do research.

- Watch out for noncompete agreements.

- Get out there and start implementing your plan.

- If you choose to have a side gig, determine your business location and the amount of time you will have outside of work with family/sleep/chores. Consider the options of sharing/renting part-time and as-needed space and acquiring a synergistic business partner.

- Build relationships when you go full time, join networking groups, and look for referrals and resources.

- Think about the pros/cons to jumping in feet first.

- Look at your personal situation, budget, and finances.

- Determine the amount of time that you have to devote to your new business.

- Consider how the skills you already have might transfer to support your new venture.

- Realize that you can work full time for months on the ramp up before you're ready for clients/income. Calculate if you can cover your expenses in that period without an income.

- Evaluate carefully before enrolling for a new degree or when taking out loans.

- Make your plan before you make commitments.

Chapter 6: Plan Your Fresh Start

- Realize that your identity can be tied to your experience. Starting over can trigger vulnerability and the need to accept that you will have a lot to learn.

- Determine what kind of help you will need. Explore the differences between coaching and consulting to find the right fit.

- Do research to determine realistic income expectations.

- Develop a plan and choose your team with intention to avoid being swept away with emotion.

- Educate family and friends to have factual/realistic expectations, so they can better support you.

- Step back and figure things out. Be willing to talk and share.

- Realize that it is a big adjustment to figure out who you are and what you want.

- Your big shift will affect your life partner, so try to get them to support you. Have realistic expectations and be sure to share your plan before acting.

- Lead the planning process, which requires talking and getting outside your comfort zone.

- Friends will tell you what they know from where they are. They might not be able to transition with you. Understanding small business can be hard for those who only know the corporate path.

- With your options, be careful not to duplicate efforts, miss opportunities, or feel paralyzed.

- Your goal is to create ease and clarity around the steps required to make money, achieve abundance, and fulfill your dream. Reduce resistance.

- Planning is like a map for a road trip, not a straitjacket. It can be changed and tweaked. Allow yourself to make intentional side trips. Enjoy the journey and avoid dead ends. Look at what others have said about how they got to where they wanted to be if you want a similar outcome.

- When others tout strategies/approaches that worked for them, compare apples with apples. Be certain that your situation is similar.

- Look at industry research for benchmarks and baselines, unmet needs, and opportunities to differentiate and disrupt.

Chapter 7: Branding

- Determine ways to differentiate your business and communicate your niche/specialty.

- Carefully name your business. Identify and brand the business with your name for a greater scope, and then name your products.

- Branding includes service. Strive to be consistent and professional. Provide quality, including your website, materials, social-media sites, photographs, and presentations.

- Don't skimp on your logo and web design. Use a professional. Get feedback and input from peers, potential clients, and mentors.

- Do it right the first time, so you don't have to redo it later.

- Vet your artist/marketing assistant/web designer. Get referrals and check their references and portfolio. Look for examples that you like and find out who did them.

- Come up with a budget and plan for branding. Prioritize spending. Don't just go for the quickest option.

- Embody your brand, including what you wear, how you act, your energy, and your style. Be yourself and don't copy others.

Chapter 8: Pick a Business Model

- Base your model on the information collected in your planning phase. Choices include one on one, group, solopreneur, small business, big company, online vs. brick and mortar, local, regional, national, international, and location-independent. Know what you ultimately want to achieve.

- Know yourself and decide where you do your best work. Decide whether you should use a home office or a shared workspace.

- Determine the tools you will need to work online and learn how to use them.

- Consider a coworking space, a shared space, incubators, coffee shops, and a rented presentation/meeting space to avoid having to sign an expensive lease.

- Get professional advice on your official business structure (e.g., a sole proprietorship, a professional partnership, a limited liability corporation, or an S Corporation).

- Think about how you will deliver your product/service (e.g., a physical or an intangible item). Know whom you are trying to reach and research delivery options.

- Determine whether your team must be on site or if they can work virtually.

- Adjust your plan as you learn to pave the way to the future.

- Consider your pricing model (e.g., free, paid (individual product or package), subscription/membership, community, and mastermind within a community).

- Determine whether you have a B2B or a B2C situation, including the option of government contracts. This will affect your business structure.

Chapter 9: Create Your Business Strategy Goals

- Do a mind dump of your priorities and list them in priority order. Focus on getting the top four priorities done in the first year. Then break down what gets done by the quarter, month, and week, and determine how these priorities are incorporated into your daily life.

- Your priorities list is a fluid document. It will be constantly updated and tweaked as your business changes.

- After you've set the strategy, think about execution and creating goals and tasks. This can be the fun part!

- Keep your focus on the outcome, whom you serve, and what change you want to see in the world.

- Identifying strategic goals helps you avoid wasting time/money/energy, increases satisfaction, gets outcomes faster, reduces clutter/overwhelm, and keeps you fixed on your target like a heat-seeking missile.

- It can be hard for subject-matter experts to realize that they need help sooner rather than later. Don't wait until you're drowning. Get qualified help, not just the easiest to find or the cheapest.

- The shift may require a change in your personal approach, so be willing to listen, adapt, and receive.

- You may have to shift plans because market conditions change.

- Understand the difference between a roadmap and a strategy. Strategies and milestones are like annual, quarterly, monthly, and weekly building blocks.

- Determine the bigger picture and the current snapshot and understand how to get from here to there. Use strategies and milestone-setting to drill down and be intentional.

- Factor in time management and task completion, like looking at mile markers along the route rather than at a final destination.

- Break targets into smaller component tasks and look for cyclicality.

- Think about how you're used to being reviewed (e.g., on individual tasks or tasks related to the big picture). Consider both tactical and strategic approaches.

Chapter 10: Sustain and Monitor

- Consider how to keep your name out there and remain current while figuring out all the behind-the-scenes issues.

- Think about monitoring to keep and track data from the beginning. Consider what metrics you'll need later.

- Keep in mind the impact you want to make. Be mission-driven.

- Continually work *on* the business as well as *in* it.

- Plan how you will get clients. Determine how many clients at which price points you will need to reach your revenue target and target number of customers/month.

- Know your conversion rate, and track each of your products/services/offerings to know what percentage of revenue they contribute (e.g., growth needs, unprofitable situations, and future promotion options).

- Plan for your source of income. Track your pipeline to create a constant flow of clients (e.g., joint ventures and speaking engagements). Look at your milestones and take steps to convert them.

- Know how to switch hats (e.g., four days doing the work and one day doing administration, following up, planning, tracking, billing, and regrouping). Outsource some but not all tasks.

- Recognize that a start-up can be seven days a week, and not 9-5, especially when ramping up. Plan to avoid burnout and set boundaries. Have clear expectations in contracts and with teams. Don't overpromise.

- Look ahead at how you want to spend your time. Corporate life might not have had boundaries. Make this the life you want. You shouldn't be continually exhausted.

- Be willing to shift/pivot, restart, fly, and repeat. It's not a one-time process. You will experience constant reinvention and restart in a cyclical pattern. Restarting and pivoting aren't failures. They are ways to adapt. Learn to cultivate resiliency. Roadmaps aren't immutable. They are constantly evolving.

- Don't base your expectations on your parents' experiences. Ups and downs will happen because the world has changed.

- Build pipelines to keep a flow of incoming projects, partners, and resources.

- Pick a starting point and let it evolve. Be fluid and go with it. Expect to evolve and mutate. Make shifts for what works for you and your market.

- Build relationships that will sustain your shift. Play a long game.

- Tracking tools differ by business, so look at the metrics for your conversion rate and understand your pipeline.

- Know what is and isn't working for monitoring. Get feedback and look for common threads. You can be mistaken, so ask. Stop doing what doesn't work sooner rather than later.

- Constant refinement and feedback are essential.

- Stay in touch to nurture future connections. Keep track of people and their needs, keep building your list, collect data, use your existing network to get feedback, and find ways to stay in regular contact.

Chapter 11: Evaluate and Modify

- When something isn't working, change sooner rather than later. Look at what isn't working and why. Determine whether you need a minor adjustment or a complete course change.
- Adapt your mindset. Things won't be perfect from day one.
- Realize that, even with transferable skills, there will be insecurity and a learning curve. It took time to become proficient at what you used to do, and it will require time to get good at the new work.
- Seek mastery. What worked in a corporate environment might not work now, so accept and adjust, and look for alternatives. Ask for help from mentors, peers, your team, and your coach. Don't try to do it all on your own.
- Realize that you wouldn't have immediate mastery if you took another corporate job, so give yourself time to grow into new responsibilities.
- Consider doing something similar to your current corporate job as a bridge while you put your roadmap into action to get where you want to go.
- Even with a roadmap, things will surprise you. React in real time and revise with research.
- Look at the obstacles (e.g., ego, momentum, and your willingness to try and fail and reinvent). Stop and pivot when it isn't working.

- Shifts are like having to go around road construction. Keep your ultimate destination in mind even when the route changes.

- Don't get emotionally tied to a particular approach. Be willing to let go and pivot. Plan to pivot.

Chapter 12: Put It All Together and Get Started!

- It's time to start your plan!

About the Author

SANDRA HUGHES is the founder of Integrated Lives, LLC d/b/a Life Reinvented, giving new and early-stage entrepreneurs the tools to turn big visions into profitable businesses with confidence and ease. She is an author and a course and program creator. She is an advisor to several nontech start-ups. She received her MBA from Santa Clara University with a concentration in Leading People and Organizations and her BA in Political Science from Wellesley College.

Sandra has comprehensive retail experience. She spent 12 years at Gap both domestically and in the United Kingdom in the real estate department. As Property Director for Gap in the UK, she was a key member of the executive team that formulated and executed the successful store-expansion strategy in the 1990s, including putting the Gap store in Piccadilly Circus where it sat for over 20 years and appeared in tourist pictures, television series, movies, and postcards, giving the brand unparalleled marketing exposure.

Today, Sandra is passionate about creating a supportive environment for aspiring and early-stage entrepreneurs. With 30-plus years' experience in building businesses, leading teams, and mentoring, she has developed extensive skills in strategic planning, complex negotiations, hiring, mentoring, and building relationships inside and outside of organizations. She has used these skills on an international level by asking the right questions in order to understand the problems before strategizing the best solutions.